MEETING JESUS

MEETING JESUS

Inspiring stories of
modern-day evangelism

By

Howard Webber

First published in 2010 by
Shield Books
© The Salvation Army
UK Territory Literary Unit
101 Newington Causeway
London SE1 6BN

ISBN 978-0-85412-823-5

All Bible quotations are from the *New International Version* unless
otherwise stated

Cover design by Jonathan Carmichael

SHIELD
BOOKS
© The Salvation Army
United Kingdom Territory with
the Republic of Ireland

This book is dedicated to
Judy my wife,
and
my five children,
Christopher,
Sarah,
Naomi,
Stephanie &
Susannah,
with thanks
for their sacrifice and support

My Thanks

I thank God for the privilege of knowing all the people mentioned
in this book and am indebted to them for all that knowing them
and being a part of their lives has meant to me.
A number of them have gone to Heaven to be with the Lord Jesus,
whom they came to know and love. This is the purpose behind all
we do and the ultimate hope and longing we have for everyone.

In particular I would like to thank
Dennis Furlong
Sonia Woolley
Nancy Lawton
Rudi and Lesley Pilsel
Pauline Boston
Janet Boston
Keith Goodall
Geoff Gerlach
Frederick Cornelius
Wayne Hardy
Andy Blastland

for reading through what I have written about them, checking it for
accuracy, correcting any errors in my record of events, and allowing
me to use their real names.

Contents

Foreword

'Anything God has ever done, he can do now. Anything God has ever done anywhere, he can do here. Anything God has ever done for anyone, he can do for you.' This quote by A. W. Tozer perhaps summarises the essence of this book by Howard Webber. It focuses our attention on the living God, whose power still staggers our imagination. While we celebrate what God has done in the past, it confirms that God is still at work, transforming lives, speaking into the human situation with words of challenge, comfort and grace. These life stories will convince us that the God who 'moved into our neighbourhood' is very busy in house-to-house, heart-to-heart visitation.

The people described in Howard's book are real, flesh and blood people. Their lives are different, their circumstances vary, but they are all in need of Christ. Many encounters end positively, a few end tragically. However, most of the people whose stories are told in *Meeting Jesus* would testify that their faith has never been misplaced. The God who saves, keeps.

Howard Webber believes that 'the greatest need is not the gift of evangelism but rather a burden for the lost'. He modestly confesses, 'I do not have the gift of evangelism, but I do have a longing, burdened heart.' The preaching, teaching and visitation aspects of his ministry are extremely focused, yet we see that these are not merely the responsibilities of a conscientious Salvation Army officer. We are seeing the heart of the man. In truth? We are seeing the heart of Jesus. Oh, to care like that!

Commissioner Linda Bond
Territorial Commander
Australia Eastern Territory

Chapter 1

Rainbow Through The Rain

We had only been in our new corps (church) six weeks when I was rushed into hospital with meningitis. We were already struggling. We had three children under 20 months, a 9-year-old daughter and an 11-year-old son fighting a life-threatening illness. The quarters (manse) we had moved into was subsiding and the corps was in a very poor state, having lost a number of leaders and seen its congregation diminish substantially. They needed what we didn't possess to save it from its continuing decline.

Fortunately, the meningitis was viral and within a week I was able to see and hear properly again, though I remained in hospital. The doctors said that I would not be left with brain damage, though friends have since suggested otherwise!

So it was that, after I had been in hospital for a week, Joy brought Andrew, her 11-year-old son – a junior soldier (junior member) of the corps – in his wheelchair to visit me; he was there for his regular hydrotherapy treatment in the hospital pool. Andrew had been diagnosed with cancer behind the eye when he was 21 months old and the radiotherapy treatment destroyed the sight in that eye. He then developed cystic fibrosis. His little life of continuing health problems had been one big struggle, yet he was amazingly positive and fun-loving.

There he sat in his wheelchair, smiling cheekily at me and whispering something to his mum which I couldn't hear. I asked what the joke was and Joy replied, 'He thinks that it is so funny that, normally, it is the captain who is dressed and he who is in pyjamas when the captain visits, but today you are in your pyjamas and he is dressed and visiting you.' It was 4.30 pm.

The following morning, just after 9 am, still weak and a little muddled, I was somewhat surprised to open my eyes after a catnap and see Joy and her husband Dennis at the end of my bed.

'What are you doing here so early in the morning?' I asked.

'Andrew's dead!' they blurted out as they both started to weep. I was devastated. I just didn't know what to say. I couldn't believe what I was hearing. They then told me that Andrew had developed breathing problems in the early hours, as had happened numerous times before; that they had tried desperately to clear his airways as they had done before, then had put him in the car and rushed him to the hospital where the medics did all they could to save him, all to no avail. He died at 4.30 am, exactly 12 hours after the lovely visit he had made to me. I felt so helpless. I was numb with shock. I prayed for and with them, but hardly knew what to say to God.

I came out of the hospital a week later on the day of Andrew's funeral. Because of our situation neither my wife nor I could attend. I sat in the sunshine in the garden in my dressing gown feeling dreadful that I couldn't even be at the hall (church) supporting the family, never mind conducting the service like I should and would have done. An officer (minister) from our area headquarters took that responsibility. Yet despite the good reasons for me being stuck where I was I felt wretched.

It was another month before I was well enough to commence work and so began my once-a-month visit to Andrew's parents. They were lovely people and I enjoyed their company. Joy was a Salvationist and, while Dennis believed in the existence of God, he was yet to discover Jesus. They had one younger son, Mark. On my visits they would talk about Andrew, there would be tears but there would also be humour and other conversation. All the time my heart bled for them. I longed to tell them how much Jesus loved them and shared their sorrow, but I held back, I just couldn't. Despite his sufferings, my 11-year-old son was still alive; their 11-year-old son was dead. They always let me pray with them before I left and many was the time that I drove home with tears running down my face, pleading with God to do something, feeling totally helpless and inadequate.

On one occasion, when Joy had gone into the kitchen to make some tea for us, Dennis suddenly turned to me and said, 'I could never join The Salvation Army!' I was taken aback and replied that I had never ever suggested that he might. However, I was intrigued by his statement and asked him why he felt like that, to which he replied, 'I am not a heavy drinker, but I do like an occasional pint and don't see anything wrong with it.'

I replied, 'There isn't anything wrong with the occasional pint; we know that Jesus drank, he drank wine while John the Baptist, for good religious reasons, never drank any alcohol. It was never an issue between them. As for joining The Salvation Army, I don't know that that is what God wants for you. I don't know whether he would have you be a Salvationist, a Baptist, a Methodist, an Anglican, a Pentecostal, or what. In fact, there is only one thing I am absolutely certain of when it comes to God and you,' I added, and then I waited.

'What is that?' he eventually asked after what seemed a very long silence.

'A deep, intimate, personal relationship with you,' I replied. Again silence followed, to be broken only by Joy returning from the kitchen chatting, with the tray laden with tea and biscuits. He said no more and neither did I. Conversation on that subject ended and was never returned to, much to my disappointment.

It was six months later that Dennis told me, again in Joy's absence, that there was a question that he had always wanted to ask someone like me (I wondered what he meant by that), but feared he might be thought foolish if he did. Hesitantly, he began by restating a fact that he had shared with me on many occasions, how Andrew had been rushed into the Intensive Care Unit of the local hospital lots of times during his brief life and how, after work, he would go up and sit with him through the evening, so that Joy, who had been there all day, could go home and give their other son some attention.

'I would stay from 6 o'clock or so to 10 or 11 o'clock at night. The evening would be long. On many an occasion Andrew was unconscious and just lay there, attached to the bleeping monitor and sometimes a drip feed. The duty sister would often come and sit and chat, or bring me a cup of coffee and perhaps a snack. There were occasions when Andrew was the only patient in the Intensive Care Unit and I would sense the sister approaching me to see how I was, only to look round and discover that there was no one there. Yet, when I turned again to Andrew, I still had the strange feeling that someone was close behind me. It happened a number of times through the years and the question that I have always wanted to ask someone has been,' he paused, 'do you think that it was God?'

Wow! That was totally unexpected. It was as if I had been standing at a red traffic light for months and then, without giving me an amber first, God had switched the light inside me straight from red to beaming, bright green! 'Yes, it was God, Dennis!' I exclaimed in what was, in effect, a verbal knee-jerk.

I had no right to say it. I had not experienced what he had experienced or checked out the precise details of his experience. My reply should surely have been, 'It could well have been God,' or, 'It might have been God.' It was only having said what I said that I then asked him to tell me more about the experience. In response, Dennis went on to describe the most wonderful sense of peace which he felt on these occasions, even though on some occasions that peace would come upon him at the same time that he was in tears, breaking his heart, wondering whether this time his boy would pull through. I asked him how long these experiences lasted and he told me that sometimes the experience would be fleeting, at other times it would last quite a while before evaporating.

'Do you know, Dennis, that God created us all to have that peace as a permanent experience? God's desire is for everyone in the world to live in that experience. There is only one thing that stops us. Did you know that there is only one thing that stops you knowing that peace as a permanent thing?' I asked.

'And what is that?' he responded.

I swallowed hard and felt my heart skip a beat. It is the thing I find hardest to say to anyone. I took a big breath, 'It's your sin.'

His eyes looked startled. 'My sin?' he asked.

In my heart I cried out 'help!' to God.

4

'Yes, your sin. I don't mean that you are a murderer, a thief or a rapist. In fact, having got to know you, Dennis, I have learnt a lot from you. There are many ways in which you are a far better man than I am. In fact I think you are a better husband and a better father than I am. The only difference is that I am forgiven.'

He sat there quiet and bemused.

'Dennis, forget for a moment what you believe or don't believe. I want to ask you a question. Tell me, say theoretically, what do you think would be the greatest sin, to break God's greatest commandment or a lesser one?'

'To break the greatest one,' he replied.

'When someone asked Jesus what was the greatest commandment, he replied that it was to, "Love the Lord your God with all your heart and with all your soul and with all your mind and with all your strength" [Matthew 22:36-37]. I don't know of anyone who loves God like that. I am a believer, I love God more today than I did when I committed myself to him, but I know I don't love him as he loves me, I know I don't love him as I should, as he commands. Logic tells me that I commit the greatest of sins and that that makes me the greatest of sinners.

'St Paul said, "Christ Jesus came into the world to save sinners – of whom I am the worst" [1 Timothy 1:15]. That baffled me for some time, Dennis, because he said "of whom *I am* the worst", not "*I was*, in the past, when I was encouraging the cold-blooded murder of Christians", but "*I am* the worst, at this present time, when I am doing all I can for God and suffering so much for Jesus Christ!"

'The Bible says that we have all sinned and the fact is that we are all the worst of sinners. If only everyone could realise that and realise also that, however much we desire to and however much we try, we can never love God as we should and that our only hope of being put right with him and having all our sins wiped from our record would be for him to wipe them away.

'So much did God love us and want us to be at one with him that he made that possible by sending Jesus, his only Son, to live a pure and perfect life of pure and perfect love. Only he deserves Heaven, but he went and died on the cross and shed his blood and went through the agony of having all our sins loaded on him and all the responsibility for them placed on his account so that our record could be wiped clean. It is a gift earned by Jesus Christ with you in mind and all you have to do to make it yours is claim it. See yourself as you really are and as God sees you, and confess that truth to God. Then ask his forgiveness and accept that his Son Jesus died for you, to be your Saviour, and you will be saved and have that peace permanently.'

Little more was said, it was getting late, I prayed for them and left.

What a pleasant surprise it was to see Dennis arrive, with Joy, at the evening meeting (service) on Sunday, two days later. He looked different, but then again it was February and it was very cold, maybe that had reddened his complexion. At the conclusion of the message I made an appeal for anyone wanting to receive salvation and accept Jesus as their Saviour to come forward. The words had hardly left my lips when Dennis was on his way to the front.

I presumed that he had come forward to seek that which we had shared on Friday evening. Only after the meeting, when we spoke together, did I discover the truth. He had felt a longing, which he couldn't explain, to make a public declaration about what he had already done. After I left their house two evenings earlier, Dennis and Joy had gone to bed (probably exhausted by my visit) and fallen asleep almost immediately. Sometime in the early hours Dennis woke up and became restless, troubled and disturbed as he pondered his life and the many experiences he had had as well as our discussion the previous evening. With a yearning to have that peace he had tasted, he got out of bed and knelt beside it while Joy, oblivious, slept on. He confessed his sin and his need of the Saviour and received Christ into his heart. In fact, so blissful was the experience of Christ's presence that he remained on his knees until dawn.

I was deeply moved at what he told me and asked if he would tell the congregation about it the following week. Everyone in the hall knew of his little boy's years of suffering and that made this statement which Dennis made, 'I never, ever realised just how much God loves me,' so moving. So profound was Dennis's life-changing experience that, when he became a soldier (member) – yes, he was convinced that that was what God wanted, and that giving up his occasional drink was nothing compared to what he now had – Joy asked if she could retake her vows and recommit her life to Christ.

'I've been a Salvationist all my life, but I haven't got what Dennis has got,' she said. I agreed to her request. Again, I asked him to speak in the meeting on the special day when he was enrolled as a soldier and he agreed. He worked in an office for the railway and he loved steam trains. He was an enthusiast.

He told us all how he had taken his son Mark out for the day with a group of railway enthusiasts. They travelled up north. He explained something of the mind of the steam-train enthusiast, and how they were all waiting in a stationary carriage for a particular steam locomotive to pass by. Someone at the end of the train gave the shout that it was approaching and everyone rushed to the side of the train, reaching out of the window holding the microphones of their tape recorders to 'catch' the particular sound that that particular steam engine made. He told how he saw such enthusiasm in a different light now and how we Christians have even more reason to get excited over what we have compared to their enthusiasm for mere steel and steam.

He also mentioned an exhibition they visited while at the railway centre, where they had seen a series of photographs showing an old steam engine which had been shunted into a siding and left there for decades. As a result, it was in a state of decay, with weeds and trees growing up under and around it. The local railway enthusiasts' club had decided to save and renovate it, and the pictures showed them clearing the undergrowth, chopping down the trees and then having the decaying monster towed out of the siding to a shed. Other photos showed the volunteers cleaning off rust, replacing parts, scraping and sanding, riveting and welding. After looking at the photographs, everyone walked out from the centre to the track and there, gleaming in all its glorious colours in the sunshine, was the finished product, looking like new.

'As I looked at those photographs and that shiny locomotive, I thought how like my life story its story was,' Dennis said, adding, 'I was like that old engine, in a siding, going nowhere, rusting, in need of restoration. No one standing by that railway track could believe the transformation of that loco. It was as new. That's what I feel Jesus has done with me. He has changed me and made me a new person. I am not the man I was and nothing that I might have ever tried could have changed me, only Jesus.'

This was a pivotal experience in my walk with the Lord, with lessons that have had a lasting effect upon my understanding and ministry. I realised that there is more going on in people than one can ever detect. God was at work in Dennis and had Dennis wondering about him and the encounters that he had with him in the Intensive Care Unit long before I arrived on the scene. Other people in the corps, with their kindness and encouragement, had been revealing the love of God to Dennis long before I met him. One can be watering a growing seed deep in the earth and not know it, as it has yet to see the light of day and reveal itself. Men are far less likely to share their hearts than women and will often give out signals that would have an observer believing that they give little thought to spiritual things, when they do.

Faithfulness in prayer is key. Whatever we do or try to do for God, the work is the Lord's. We must not lose heart, passion or the desire to see fruit, but nor should we try to force God's hand. We must wait on the Lord, attentive and ready for when he acts. 'The wind blows wherever it pleases. You hear its sound, but you cannot tell where it comes from or where it is going' (John 3:8). The Holy Spirit will often give truths, recorded in Holy Scripture, to a person long before he or she has ever heard of or read the passage. So it was with Dennis and his reflection on his experience of the locomotive's transformation. He had yet to read, 'If anyone is in Christ, he is a new creation; the old has gone, the new has come!' (2 Corinthians 5:17).

Chapter 2

Success Despite Failure

Life was very busy and pressured in the corps and in our home. I had struggled to visit everyone recorded on our membership rolls (soldiers and adherent members) and, like the shepherd seeking the one lost sheep, I had just one more to find, a single woman. By her position on the roll she was an older, single woman, whom none of the local officers (elders) seemed to know. She could not have attended for years, they told me.

I went to the address recorded by her name on the roll. The couple that came to the door told me that they had lived in the house for several years and that the previous tenant had been a widow not a spinster. So I went next door to enquire, to no avail; then the next house to that, and the next to that, gradually moving along the street. None of those who answered their doors remembered the woman I was looking for or knew anything of her. Eventually, having travelled some distance from where I began, I returned to the house where I had started and commenced the same process in the opposite direction. One man who came to the door did remember the woman in question and said that she had lived there with her sister, but that it was quite some years ago since they had moved out. He didn't know where they had moved to.

Again I returned to where I had started. This time I crossed the road, went through a gate and up the garden path to the little semi-detached cottage opposite. In response to my door knocking a small woman I judged to be in her early 50s came to the door. She looked very nervous so I tried to put her at her ease with humour. I told her that I was a minister of a church, The Salvation Army, that I had moved into town in June and that slowly, like a shepherd, I have been

9

trying to account for and meet all the sheep in my flock but that there was still one, just one, that I could not find. She laughed and asked me if it was a black one! I told her how I had spent over an hour in her street and that I had confirmed that the woman I was seeking had lived with her sister in the house opposite hers, but that they had moved away and no one knew where she had gone.

The woman was bemused.

'They left there years ago,' she said, 'it must be at least eight years ago.'

'Do you know where they went?' I asked.

'Yes,' she replied.

'Yippee!' I thought.

'Go down to the end of this road,' she said, pointing with her finger, 'turn right into the main road. About half a mile on the right is a telephone box. The gate to their house is right next to the telephone box. Sorry, I don't know the number.'

'Brilliant, thanks,' I replied.

'I used to see them around, but I haven't seen them for quite some time,' she added.

'How old do you think the one I am looking for is?' I asked.

'Oh, she must be at least 80,' was her response.

As we talked together I looked into her eyes. They seemed full of kindness, but I also detected something else. Despite making her smile, I detected a sadness about her. I felt that behind her smile lay a troubled heart.

'How are *you*?' I asked.

'Oh, I'm all right,' she responded.

'Are you? Are you really all right?' She hesitated, staring into my eyes. 'Is there anything you'd like to share? Is there something troubling you?' I added. Again there was a long silence.

'You don't want to be bothered with my problems, you are very busy,' she eventually said.

'I do want to be bothered and I can always make time. I don't want to impose myself upon you or embarrass you, but if you would like me to, I could take your telephone number and, once we have got

Christmas out of the way, I could ring you and come and see you. If you change your mind and decide that you don't wish to speak to me after all, that will be OK too. What do you think?'

'I'd like that,' she said.

I took out my pocket diary and recorded her name, Nancy Lawton, her address and her telephone number. She told me a little about her children and her late husband and I then shared a little bit of my life and the troubles our family had been facing that she might empathise with. I then wished her a happy Christmas and left. I didn't share with her to gain sympathy, but to try and remove any idea (an idea that many people seem to have) that Christian ministers don't have the troubles that other mortals have and therefore can never know what other people face and go through.

Christmas was very hectic. The corps, like most churches, had a very busy programme. We then entered the new year. There were crises and emergencies to respond to and things to organise, as well as the weekly routine of visiting the people, preparing for Sunday worship and other meetings. The weeks rushed by.

In March, one of the soldiers arranged a corps social, a sort of cabaret evening to raise funds. When I arrived, various members and guests were finding seats at the beautifully decorated tables. I went and sat on a vacant chair at a table where two of our over-60 club members and a stranger were sitting. The entertainment began with various folks showing their talents and musical prowess, all very good. Then there followed an intermission and we lined up to load our plates from the mouth-watering buffet that had been set out at one end of the room. Returning to the table, we all shared in conversation and laughter. I then got talking to the stranger at the table, a small woman I judged was in her early 50s.

As we talked I was a little unsettled by the way she seemed to be looking at me with a steady gaze and the faint glimmer of a smile on her lips. At one point, while talking about families and the fact that my family could not be there, she made a remark that startled me regarding my situation. What she said, I had rarely confided outside our home.

'Where did you get that from?' I asked, puzzled. 'Who told you that?'

'You did,' she said.

'I did?' I questioned, somewhat nonplussed, having never set eyes on this lady before (or so I thought).

'Yes.'

'When?' I quizzed.

'When you came to my house,' she said with a now broad grin.

The minute those words left her lips I remembered. 'Oh no!' I exclaimed. I suddenly came over feeling very hot indeed. 'I came to your house before Christmas when I was looking for someone belonging to the Army who at one time had lived in your road.' She nodded in agreement. 'And I promised you that I would come and see you after all the Christmas busy-ness was over. I'm so, so sorry. I just don't know what to say. I don't know how I could have failed you like that. I'm sure that I wrote down your name, address and telephone number.'

'You did, in your diary,' she replied.

'I bet I know what I did,' I said taking my diary from my pocket. 'When I transferred the entries I needed from my old diary to my new one, somehow I must have failed to copy your details.' I looked at the back of the diary and sure enough there was no record of the information that Nancy had given me.

'Don't worry,' she said graciously, 'it's just one of those things. You are very busy with more important things to see to, and anyway I'm here now.'

'That's no excuse,' I replied. 'I made a promise and I didn't keep my word, and none of the other things are more important than seeing you. It may have been unintentional but there is no excuse for such carelessness, even though I can understand how I did it. I am so, so sorry. I'm amazed that you have come here after that. Do you still want me to come and see you?'

'I do, if you could find the time. The reason I came here tonight is because my friend goes to your over-60 club and I mentioned that you and I had met, and that I was confused that you had not come back to me like you promised. She spoke up for you. I told her how you lifted my spirits that day we met and that I thought there must have been a good reason why I didn't hear from you afterwards.'

We sorted out a date there and then and I visited her the following week. She told me of the ongoing emptiness she felt following the death of her husband a few years earlier. She also told me distressing things that had happened in her childhood that were still a cause of great inner pain and grief. She shared how she went regularly each Sunday morning to the local church and, although she enjoyed it and found it a comfort and felt good while she was there, she also felt that 'it all left her' as she walked out through the church door. She said she did believe in God and said her prayers regularly every morning and evening, but felt that something was missing.

I then carefully enquired as to whether anyone had told her that she could know God personally, telling her that she could know Jesus as her Saviour and her friend and that he knew all about pain, injustice, loneliness, abuse and bereavement. She had been going to church for many years but no one had talked to her in such personal terms about Jesus. She had never heard God's message of salvation through Jesus preached. We prayed together. She then told me that she didn't want to leave her church. She felt it was right to stay there but, as they did not have an evening service, she would like to join with us on Sunday evenings if that was all right with me. I said that I was more than happy for her to do that, adding that she would do both churches good and provide a link between us.

So that is what she did. It was not long before she came forward one Sunday evening to seek salvation. God transformed her. She now knew in whom she believed and the Holy Spirit gave her an assurance that she didn't have before. That which she had so long sensed within the church services she attended, she now had within her heart.

The sad thing is that, when she told her own minister about her spiritual rebirth and her attendance at our evening service, he teased her and taunted her and spoke ill of us, which hurt her. He asked her if she was being made to play a tambourine yet. She stayed with the arrangement for quite some time but, despite my encouragement for her to stay with her church and be a blessing to others there, the unpleasant and sarcastic remarks did not cease and she finally decided to leave and become a member of our corps of The Salvation Army. That was 20 years ago. She is still there and still walking with Jesus.

How gracious God is. Despite my failure, carelessness and incompetence, God gave me a second chance to reach dear Nancy. Praise God that the eternal destinies of others do not rest on our capabilities and efficiency. God tunes in to the desires of our hearts and, as long as we own up to our failures and our shortcomings and humbly accept that we forever fall short of what is needed, he can override our deficiencies. And my experience is that he not only can, but he does.

Chapter 3

Reluctant To Witness

Having tried knocking on the doors of the houses in a street during one of our outdoor services, I found that either no one came to the door or those who did didn't want to talk to me about anything. I made my way back to where the band was now playing. No one was at all interested in speaking to me and I was tired and ready for my dinner. There was a large rubbish skip in the road, and I caught sight of what, from where I stood, appeared to be a rat or small cat doing a balancing act along its far rim! I was intrigued. 'What could that be?' I wondered. It turned out to be the hair on the top of the head of a very short woman of about 70 years of age who, on reaching the end of the skip, turned and stepped off the pavement before then standing alongside the skip to watch and listen to what was going on.

I felt inclined to let her linger there, though something inside prompted me to speak to her. I pushed the prompting away, but the thought suddenly arose, 'What if this person's eternal destiny is dependent on you speaking to her at this moment?' I dismissed this thought as a piece of mental melodrama, though of course it could always be true.

The compulsion wouldn't go, so I reluctantly went and spoke to her. I discovered that she was a widow living alone in a house in the next street and was on her way home for lunch. I asked her if she knew one of our members who lived in a house on the opposite side of the road to her. She said that she didn't, so I asked her if she would like to meet the woman in question as she is such a sweet person. She said that she would love to. So we left the open-air service and walked together the few hundred yards to Queenie Hancock's home and knocked on her front door.

Queenie, also a widow and also in her 70s, came to the door in her apron. She was obviously busy getting her dinner ready, but on sight of me immediately apologised for not being at the outdoor service – something she never did anyway and I would never expect her to do. She hadn't noticed little Vera standing next to me.

'Queenie, you're in your 70s, you know full well I don't expect you to be standing out in the cold in the open air. This is Vera, she lives at number 3. She was interested in what she heard when she stopped to listen to our service and, when she told me where she lived, I asked her if she knew you. She said she didn't, so I told her what a lovely lady you were and asked her if she would like to meet you. She said, "Oh yes, I would," so here we are.'

Queenie's response truly blessed me. 'Would you like to come in and have a cup of coffee, Vera?'

I knew we had called at an inconvenient time. Queenie was about to dish out her dinner but she set that aside to offer Vera hospitality. Vera went inside, turned and thanked me and the door closed behind her.

Obviously I was not party to their conversation, and Queenie would not consider herself to be an evangelist. She would have said that she was ordinary, nothing special, despite me frequently teaching my congregation that they are all very special. She was a background person, friendly, always ready to help with coffee mornings and corps meals, etc, but that evening, as I mounted the platform and looked out at the congregation, there she was sitting with Vera. She had brought Vera with her to the evening meeting.

When it came to the sermon, I spoke of God's love in Christ and his enormous sacrifice on the cross and the need of us all to receive the forgiveness that he offers. Then I made an appeal to those who did not know God's forgiveness to reach out and respond. Little Vera didn't need to be asked twice. She came forward immediately and knelt before God and was saved that night.

Often afterwards she would testify to how that morning changed her whole life – and to think I could have missed the opportunity so easily. It leaves me wondering, too, as to how many other opportunities I have missed, opportunities that have been staring me in the face, opportunities that I have failed to see or been reluctant to respond to when prompted to do so.

Yes, we are human so we could get it all wrong and fall on our faces, but I think that often we spend too much time worrying about ourselves. May we risk the consequences of being wrong and be willing to be failures. I believe that God is calling us into the deeps – into uncharted seas – as churches and as individuals, and that too often there is a reluctance to move from the comfort of the paddling pool that we know into an ocean we have never been in before. Well, that is my testimony.

Chapter 4

Guided In The Dark

There is no more exciting life available than the Spirit-led life of a Spirit-filled person. So many times I have reluctantly stepped out into the dark like a timid, uncertain child and there discovered the most tremendous display of the power, the beauty and the light of this magnificent God of ours. I may have stepped out timidly and fearfully but the fact that, despite my feelings, I did step out has proved sufficient faith for God to respond. The Spirit may lead us in many different ways: to write that letter for no real reason that we know of to someone we have never met; to start on a venture for which we know that we haven't the qualifications or resources; to visit, 'out of the blue', that person whom we met only once by seeming chance years ago.

After a very tiring day, having got into my pyjamas and sat myself on the edge of the bed, I opened my bedside locker drawer to get some papers out for the morning. Seeing the disarray of its contents, I decided a quick tidy up was necessary before going to sleep. Among the things I found was a small, long-forgotten notebook. I could not resist flicking through its pages. There were all sorts of notes and reminders, from sermon thoughts and illustrations to things my wife, Judy, had obviously asked me to get from a shop while out on my travels.

There were also the odd name and also names with addresses. One in particular caught my attention – why I do not know. It wasn't written in block capitals or underlined, and I had no recall of the woman whose name was recorded. It was a Mrs Woolley, with an address written underneath, followed by the first lines of two hymns, a few other notes and the name of a funeral director. It seemed obvious to me that they were written down in response to the first telephone enquiry from a funeral director about conducting a funeral. Having no recall whatsoever, I presumed from the details that Mrs Woolley was the daughter of the deceased.

I sat for some time pondering this particular entry in my notebook. Then the thought occurred to me, 'Why not surprise this Mrs Woolley with a visit?' This was followed very quickly with another thought, 'How ridiculous! As if I haven't got enough to do this week. And why should I surprise someone I don't even remember? And for what purpose?' I popped the notebook back in the drawer, got into bed, switched off the light and was soon fast asleep.

The first thing that entered my head when I awoke early the following morning was that entry in the notebook. Why it should claim my interest any more than any other similar entry I had no idea, but I quietly took the book from the drawer, crept downstairs and made myself a cup of tea before settling into reading my Bible and spending some time with God in prayer. In fact, I asked him if it was anything from him and, if so, would he clarify things for me? There was no answer on that one. So, after prayer, I just popped the notebook in my jacket pocket.

It was a very busy week, with lots of things to be done, people to visit, problems to sort out. Before I knew where I was it was Friday and the thought of the notebook and that entry had long been forgotten. Normally on a Friday I would spend time in my office down at the hall, clearing administrative tasks at the same time as the weekly coffee morning took place. That way I was available should anyone coming into the building need to talk or need my help. Every hour or so I would stop what I was doing and wander down the corridor to where the 'customers' were drinking their coffee to say hello to everyone, before returning to continue wading through the pile of paperwork.

This particular Friday I had a change in my routine. I had seen an advertisement for a good quality second-hand piano for sale in one of the outlying villages some distance from our town. We desperately needed one in our young people's hall, and this one we could afford.

Friday morning was the only time and day the songster leader (choirmaster) could come with me to look at it.

So it was that we went and examined and listened to the piano, agreed to buy it and organised its delivery. I then drove back to town, dropping Charlie at his door. It was too late to go home and grab a lunchtime snack and there were a number of people in the west end of town I wanted to visit before the weekend, so I just headed in that direction.

As I drove the mile and a half to my first call, I noticed the name of one of the many roads I passed, *Frank Webb Avenue*. It rang a bell. I immediately pulled over to the kerb and stopped. I took out my notebook and looked at the entry. Sure enough, it was the road recorded in my book as being where Mrs Woolley lived. 'Mmmm,' I thought, 'is God trying to tell me something, I wonder?' I reversed my caravanette, drove down the road and parked outside the house. Beginning to think that for some reason I had been led there, I walked confidently up the garden path and knocked on the door, anticipating an answer. No one responded to my knocking. There was no one in. So I got back into my vehicle, thinking to myself, 'You deluded boy, your imagination is overactive. God obviously wasn't the one prompting you or else there would have been someone in!'

I was about to drive off when the thought came to me, 'But what if God does want you to make contact? If you leave a note and are wrong, what have you lost? But if you fail to leave a note and you were meant to make contact then it could be serious.'

I had no pages in the old notebook on which to write a note, so I rummaged through my glovebox and found an old leaflet. I wrote on the back, 'Dear Mrs Woolley, you may remember me. I conducted your mother's funeral some time ago. I just wondered how you are and wanted to remind you that, should you ever need me, please don't be afraid to give me a ring,' adding my name at the end.

I was about to add my telephone number, but it occurred to me that she might think that I wanted her to telephone me. I didn't want her to feel obliged to call. I decided that, if I was tuning into something God was already doing, she would somehow get in touch

21

with me, even if she didn't initially know where I was. On the other hand, if all that was going on in my mind was nonsense and I was wrong, I didn't want her to feel alarmed or fearful or pressured to ring me. I popped the note through the letter box and that was that. I continued with the afternoon as I had planned.

The following night, Saturday, I had a rare evening in with the family. The weather outside was stormy, with torrential rain beating against the windows. I was enjoying a welcome time playing with our three youngest children when suddenly the telephone rang. I wasn't pleased, but went and answered it anyway.

'Hello, is that the captain?'

'Yes,' I replied.

'This is Sonia.'

'Sonia?'

'Yes, you came to my house yesterday. Sonia Woolley.'

'Oh, Mrs Woolley, how lovely to hear you.'

'Have you got a minute?' she asked.

'Of course,' I replied.

'I can't get over yesterday and your visit,' she said. 'I've been thinking a lot about things this last year and I thought of going to church, but whenever I mention it to my friends at work, they either laugh and say, "You're not going all religious are you?" or they agree to go with me but never ever get around to doing so.

'I have been feeling a bit low lately. I have a lovely husband, but he doesn't understand, bless him. Also, I've been a bit unwell, so I took some time off work yesterday and went to the doctor's. My doctor's surgery is in the town centre. On my way back to the bus station I passed your hall and saw your coffee morning sign outside and suddenly remembered you and decided to come in and see if you were about and whether I could talk to you. The ladies were very nice and told me that normally you are there every Friday morning, but yesterday you would not be in at all. I was so disappointed, and after drinking my coffee I caught the bus and went back to work.

'When I got in from work in the evening, my husband was already home. Imagine my surprise when I opened the door and he said, "Hi,

Sonia, you'll never guess what, there was a note for you on the doormat from The Salvation Army when I got home." You could have knocked me over with a feather.'

I was amazed. I asked her when it was that I conducted her mother's funeral service. She told me that it wasn't her mother's, it was her aunt's, and that it was a year ago the previous May. Fifteen months had passed since last I had any contact with Sonia and then, on the very day that I sought to make contact with her, she was seeking to make contact with me. Coincidence?

'I want to try and come to the service tomorrow. Do you have an evening service?'

'Yes, we do. It's at 6.30 pm, I'll look out for you.'

'I'm very nervous, I might not make it.'

'Please don't worry. Force yourself, you won't regret it. There are some lovely people there.'

'I feel as though God brought you to my house and that he is behind all this,' she added.

'He is,' I replied. 'I have no doubts about that.'

I was nervous myself the following night as I stood in the foyer of our hall looking out for Sonia. I had no recall of her and what she looked like. I didn't know who I was looking for, yet the moment she stepped in the door I recognised her, and the sight of her brought back a host of memories that had laid dormant and out of reach until then.

I remembered how, 15 months earlier, as I prepared her aunt's funeral and listened to her telling me about what a lovely Christian woman her aunt was and what her favourite hymns were, I had wondered whether Sonia was a Christian herself. I remembered wondering how to find out in an unobtrusive, non-threatening way. I had expressed the fact that I wished I had known her aunt, that she must have been a lovely woman and tagged on the question as to what faith she, Sonia, had – what was her relationship with God? She had reacted angrily and told me not to start pushing religion down her throat (which was the last thing I wanted to do).

Had I remembered that incident, I may well have dismissed any idea of trying to make contact with her at all! I also remembered that, after the funeral, I had popped round to see how she was. She had been very close to her aunt and was very upset at the funeral. Having been clearly told off prior to the funeral, I made no mention of faith, God or anything related to religion or spiritual things. I merely expressed my concern for her, as I do with all non-church people who call on me to conduct the funeral of a loved one, adding that should she ever need any help of any kind not to hesitate to contact me, that even if she never came near our church, she still mattered to us. Apparently, she remembered that.

Sonia became a regular attender on a Sunday evening, and a few months later committed her life to Jesus and came to know him as her Saviour and friend. I discovered later, in general conversation, that, when she telephoned me on that dreadful Saturday night (weather-wise), she had walked some distance in the downpour to the nearest public telephone box – having no telephone at home – only to find that it was disconnected because of vandalism. So convicted and convinced was she that my note to her was a message from the Lord and that she had to get in contact with me, she had then walked a further half mile towards town in the pouring rain, getting soaked to the skin, to do so.

It isn't easy for us little mortals to know, in any given set of circumstances, exactly what it is God wants us to do, or whether what we are sensing is from him. Sometimes it is clear but often, in my experience, it isn't. Sometimes I have asked God for a clear and definite sign, adding the promise that I won't tell anybody else if I see his finger in the sky. But I have never seen a visible light or a finger or heard an audible voice, yet I guess that even in the dark without our being conscious of him, he does guide us. How else could such a thing as I have just described happen?

Chapter 5

Concerned Parents

In the absence of a leader or potential leader for a corps group, officers are left with one of two choices, either they close the group down, or else they lead it themselves. Although I had two people responsible for the under-7-year-old children (primary class) in the Sunday school, I had no leader for the main Sunday school. So it fell to me to lead it. It was a healthy group, with 20 children regularly attending and new children joining from outside the corps, often children of non-believers.

Sundays were very busy days, with morning worship at 10 am, followed by an outdoor service from 11.30 am until 12 noon. There was then a rush home for lunch with my wife and five children before getting back to the hall for 1.30 pm in time to greet the children as they began to arrive. It was an active and exhausting hour and, at the end of it, we would close with prayer before I hurried out the door ahead of a pursuing horde of children rushing to meet waiting parents like a scene from *The Bash Street Kids*. Once outside, I would lean against the wall as they all rushed past – shouting their goodbyes to me – into the embrace of mum or dad or into the cars of corps folk who were waiting to take them home.

On one occasion, having shouted 'go' and led them Pied Piper style through the door, I looked over their heads as I wearily leaned on the wall and saw a young woman whom I hadn't seen before staring at me rather strangely. The rush ended and there were just a few stragglers still to leave as I wandered across and introduced myself. Her name was Lesley and she told me that she was the mother of Annie and Tom whom she had brought to the Sunday school that day for the first time.

I was curious to know what had made her bring the children to our Sunday school, and she told me two things. Firstly, she was concerned for what she felt was the lack of proper moral teaching in the schools these days, adding that she was a schoolteacher who had temporarily given up teaching so that she could bring up her family. The second reason was that she had always had a warmth towards and great respect for The Salvation Army and its practical Christianity. I asked her if she had ever been to a Salvation Army service and she said that she hadn't.

'Why don't you give it a try on a Sunday morning? Our meetings are at 10 am until about 11.15 am, and God does come and bless us. Of course you might not like it, but it is relaxed. Just feel free to get up and go if it's not to your liking. I promise I won't cry.'

Lesley smiled,

'Well, actually that's not true, but I won't do it until I get home,' I added.

Now Lesley added a look to her smile that seemed to say, 'I think that you're an idiot,' though of course it might not have been what she was thinking at all!

It was a delight the following Sunday morning to look down from the platform and see Lesley sitting there. When the meeting was over my wife and I stood at the door to shake hands with the congregation and the first to greet us was Lesley with her head down. I was going to ask her if she had enjoyed the service but, as I had conducted it, I was fearful that it might look as if I were fishing for compliments, so I asked her how she was instead.

She looked up, her eyes full of tears, and just said, 'I've come home,' before grabbing and pulling on the door handle and rushing out and across the grass.

I looked back at my wife, asking her, 'I wonder what that was about?'

For the next few weeks Lesley attended morning worship on her own, bringing her two children to Sunday school in the afternoons. We had snippets of conversation, but it wasn't easy to talk with so many other people around, so one Sunday morning I asked if she would like me to visit and whether she thought her husband would mind.

'Oh, I would love you to,' she replied. 'I've told my husband all about you and he'd love to meet you, too,' she added.

'You've told him all about me? In that case I think I'll take a rain check on the visit,' I quipped.

Although I try and hide it, I'm always nervous when I meet someone for the first time, but I needn't have worried. I had a great time together with Lesley and her husband, Rudi, with all sorts of questions about faith and belief and The Salvation Army. Rudi had been brought up as a Roman Catholic, his father having come to the UK from Poland. He shared with me his concerns regarding Catholicism and the things that he just could not accept about it. Not wanting to be critical of another faith, when Rudi talked about some of the ways he felt that the church failed to practice what it preached, I shared the fact that my church wasn't perfect either, that there were things in it that troubled me, but that the focus of my life was Jesus. This apparently warmed him rather than put him off.

At the end of the afternoon together, they allowed me to pray for them and their family, after which Rudi said, 'I will be there on Sunday morning, but Lesley won't.'

'Why won't Lesley be there?' I enquired.

They immediately looked at each other and together replied, 'Jack!' and then laughed.

I didn't get the joke. They went on to explain that they had a third child, an 18-month-old whom I hadn't seen and who hadn't been mentioned. He was hyperactive. I was still puzzled.

'You would not want Jack in a church service,' chuckled Rudi.

'No way,' agreed Lesley, laughing and nodding her head.

They went on to explain that Jack needed very little sleep, had a very short concentration span, would not sit still and would guarantee disruption in any church service he went to. Annie and Tom would be no trouble, but Jack…? There was no way they could bring Jack to the corps. They would take turns to come while the other one cared for Jack at home.

27

'Look, bring him. It really is no problem. If he is unsettled or noisy we'll get used to it,' I said. I could tell they were not convinced by the knowing looks they exchanged.

I continued, 'I am looking forward to the day when our church is so focused on seeing people come in and find Christ that, even if the service is ruined for them and they get nothing from it, they will go home praising God because you were there and their concern is more for you and your spiritual welfare and eternal destiny than their own comforts and preferences. I have to say that we're not there yet by a long chalk, but I believe it's where we ought and need to be. If Jack does play you up and embarrass you, and should someone give you a cold, judgmental stare, don't let it upset you. Please don't get up and leave. That person has a problem. Please find it in your heart to forgive them.'

Sunday morning came and there were Rudi and Lesley, together with Annie, Tom and Jack and, true to form, Jack would not sit still. Poor Lesley, how she struggled with him. Jack loved our chairs. They were in regimented rows, each chair attached by a link to the next one, creating a tunnel between the legs that extended the length of the row – something someone six foot five inches tall who doesn't often crawl would not have thought of.

Jack loved it. He crawled the length of one row, came out into the aisle and then crawled under the next row. He and not I had the full attention of everyone. It was not the congregation that had the problem in terms of responding in a Christlike manner to Jack, it was me! From where I was standing, I felt that I might as well have not preached a word. Hours of preparation and prayer for what?

But God was at work in it all. They came together as a family each Sunday morning after that and then one or other parent would come to evening worship, what we call the salvation meeting. It was one Sunday evening, some six weeks after first attending worship, that first Rudi, then the following week Lesley, sought and received God's love and forgiveness in Jesus. They themselves are officers serving in The Salvation Army today.

Chapter 6

A Prodigal Returns

We had a club for pensioners, an over-60 club, which met each Tuesday afternoon. They had lots of fun and laughter, guest speakers, day coach trips and holidays, in addition to quiet times, hymns and prayers. Consequently, there was an exciting buzz about the place and new people were regularly added to the numbers. In the absence of a leader it fell to me to lead this group for a few years.

A 79-year-old named Grace Sykes joined us. I discovered that she and her husband lived about two miles away and came into town on the bus each Tuesday afternoon. He would leave her by the door while he wandered round the town for 90 minutes before returning to accompany her on the bus home. I asked her once why he didn't come in and find out whether it was something that he might like, but all that she said was that he wouldn't. Some time passed, then one Tuesday during the meeting I noticed Grace crying. I went and sat with her when the meeting finished and she told me that Alf, her husband, had been rushed into hospital having had a heart attack, and that she had thought that she was going to lose him. Although he was improving, she was still very worried.

I then asked her whether he might appreciate a visit as I was visiting the hospital later that week.

'No, I don't think so,' she replied. I was puzzled and enquired as to the reason why, when we had not ever spoken to one another and he hardly knew me.

'It's a long story and you are very busy,' she said.

'I am never that busy and I would love to hear it if you are willing to share it.'

29

She started to cry again, 'Well, years ago both Alf and I belonged to the large church up West Street. We grew up in Christian homes and we met at the church when we were young and that is where we were married. All our friends were in that church and we were very happy. We both worked hard there and Alf was an elder as well as being responsible for the Boys Brigade Unit. We were both Sunday school workers, too. One day one of the other elders said something very unkind to Alf, something quite derogatory, accusing him of something he had not done, something that put a big question mark over his honesty and integrity. He was mortified. It broke him and he left and became a very bitter man when it came to anything to do with church and religion. From that time on he has had no time for it at all, although he still says he believes in God and regularly prays and reads his Bible.'

'When did all this happen?' I asked.

'Oh, it must be all of 40 or more years ago now,' she replied. 'He has never stepped inside a church since and has even had it written into his will that, when he dies, his body is not to be taken into a church.'

We both sat in silence. She was a lovely woman, very small, thin and fragile-looking. She walked with a stick, not too steadily. I looked at the lines in her face, some I am sure etched there by the years of sorrow and, as I looked into her eyes, my heart ached for her and for her husband, even though I didn't know him.

'I would still like to visit him, if I may.'

'Well, if you do, please don't get upset if he is abrupt and rude to you. Don't take it personally. It isn't you. He really is a lovely, caring man. Oh, and do try not to mention religion or the church.' Grace then allowed me to pray with her and then some dear soul, who had stayed behind to offer her a lift, drove her home.

When I next visited the hospital I left the visiting of Alf until last. I found concentrating on the other people I visited difficult because all the time I was wondering what my reception would be when I met Alf. I also wondered what I would talk about.

On arriving at the ward I was led to a side room where Alf was lying on his bed. We shook hands and I introduced myself and asked how he was and what the current situation regarding his health was. I then asked him about his family and what he had done before he retired, carefully avoiding anything to do with God, Jesus, church or religion.

He asked me about my family, myself and my past. I replied very cautiously, resisting my natural tendency to tell him how I came to know Jesus. He was gracious and polite and we shared some humour. I sensed a real warmth exuding from him. I also found his eyes fascinating. They were a light blue, like coloured glass, and they shimmered. All the time he was looking at me they seemed to be pulsating ever so slightly. After some 30 minutes I told him how much I had enjoyed meeting him and he thanked me and I departed.

When Tuesday came round, there was Grace, looking much better, beckoning me over to speak with me.

'Hello Grace, you look so much better. How's Alf?'

'Much better. They have moved him to a convalescent home owned by the railway works where he used to work. He was so happy when I saw him after your visit. He was so pleased that you visited him.'

'Thank goodness,' I smiled.

'He said that there was only one disappointment,' she added.

'What was that?' I asked.

'Well, he said that a great yearning welled up in him as you talked with him, a longing for you to pray with him, and that he was so disappointed because you left without doing so.'

I must have shown my shock. I always offer to pray when I visit, even if the person is a stranger to me or a non-believer. But I made a point on this occasion of not offering to pray for obvious reasons.

'It's OK, Captain. I explained to him that I had spoken to you about how things are, and he understood. He felt you had a genuine concern for him and he felt something stir inside. In fact he shed a tear while he was talking to me.'

Alf was some time in the convalescent home, somewhere in Devon I believe. I visited Grace from time to time as she could never travel the 200 plus miles to see him. Eventually he came home and some months later, one Tuesday over lunch, before they caught their bus to town, he informed Grace that he was coming to the club. And so he did. He came in the door with Grace on his arm and everyone gave him a warm welcome and expressed how pleased they were that he had recovered. As a result he continued to attend. Weeks passed, when suddenly one Sunday over lunch he announced to Grace, 'We are going to catch the bus to church tonight!'

'What church?' she asked.

'The Salvation Army church,' he replied.

They became a regular part of the Sunday evening congregation. Then one Sunday, after I had given the message and made an appeal for anyone to publicly express their desire to accept Christ as their Saviour and to be his follower, these two elderly people rose to their feet and, holding each other's hands and their walking sticks, they slowly walked to the front to be prayed for.

They became members and wanted to wear uniform to declare their new-found faith. I remember Alf's testimony the Easter Sunday night that he and his wife made their promises of commitment to Christ. He explained how more than 40 years earlier he had been deeply hurt by a member of his church and that he had foolishly taken his eyes away from Jesus.

'If only I had kept my eyes on the cross and seen how Jesus bore pain for me, took false accusations and injustice upon himself for me and never retaliated, and never gave up on me. I, on the other hand, let him down and deserted him and was unwilling to suffer hurt, false accusations and injustice for him. All through the years I have continued to pray and read my Bible and do good to people, thinking I could be a Christian without going to church. In fact I thought I was a lot better than those who do go to church. How wrong I was. I wasn't right in my heart. I was bitter and angry and I didn't love my enemies and I wasn't right with God. I am so pleased that, despite that, God never gave up on me, and I am also so pleased to be standing here making these promises tonight. I have wasted more than 40 years of my life. I want to give God all the days I have left.'

Though elderly, with limited mobility and unable to do much physically, both Alf and Grace Sykes made a bigger impact upon the corps than they were ever aware. Warmth and love shone from their faces and words of encouragement flowed from their lips to everyone who came near to them. You could never leave their company without feeling better for having spent time with them, even if it was only a few minutes.

A year later we had a group of cadets (trainee ministers) with us from the training college in London, conducting an Easter campaign (mission). On the Good Friday morning we erected a cross in the centre of a room at the corps and gathered round it to consider the events of that first Good Friday. After a few hymns about Christ's sacrificial death, there followed a time of silence when opportunity was given for anyone to speak regarding their thoughts or to sing a song or play a tape focused on the Crucifixion. Alf slowly rose to his feet and spoke directly to the young cadets, 'I can't wait until Sunday. It's the day when our Lord rose from the dead and gave us all hope. The day is also the anniversary of when I became a soldier of Jesus Christ. This year has been the best year of my life. I have learnt more of the Bible this past year than I did all the time I attended church before. God has been so good to me. Dear young people, I am in my 80s now. I don't know how long God has for me here, but I want to tell you, you will be let down, you will know disappointments, you will get hurt by people who should know better, but keep your eyes on the cross. Don't give up. Don't leave like I did. Keep your eyes fixed on Jesus. Nothing compares to living for Jesus.' He sat down. All eyes were on Alf. His glassy blue eyes seemed to be shimmering more than normal.

Easter Sunday morning at 8 am the telephone in the hallway at home rang.

The call was from the hospital, from Alf and Grace's daughter. 'Dad had a heart attack this morning. Mum wanted you to know,' she said.

When I announced at the beginning of morning worship what had happened, a murmur of shock went across the congregation and the cadets looked upset. I visited Alf later that day. He was comfortable. He gradually improved over the following days. About a week later, he was sat up, with his glasses on, reading his Bible.

'How are you, Alf?'

'A lot better, a lot better. I decided to read the whole of the New Testament again. Already I've read the Gospels and Acts and I'm halfway through Romans. It's great.'

We talked together. I told him about what he had missed on Easter Sunday, how shocked and sad the cadets and everyone else were at what had happened to him and the effect that his words on Good Friday had had on us all. He talked of what he wanted to do when he got better, 'God willing,' he added. I prayed for him before I left. It was a precious time. I had no idea that it would be the last time I saw him. In the night that followed, Alf had another, much bigger heart attack and the Lord carried him off to be with him. I lost a dear friend.

Who can measure the impact of the life of one person, totally surrendered to God for even a short time? We often think that it is what we do and how much we do that has the most significance for the Kingdom when it is what we are that matters most and makes the biggest impact on others.

Chapter 7

Motherly Interest

The Easter campaign that the cadets conducted at our corps lasted ten days, leading up to its planned climax on the Easter Sunday. Prior to the visit, the training college officer who was to lead the group met with some of our people and myself to put together a programme, which would include door-to-door visitation, open-air meetings, seminars and other meetings. Prior to their visit, much prayer went up to God from the corps and from the cadets whom we were yet to meet. They were a very lively, enthusiastic group who were passionate about what they were doing.

While conducting a meeting in the open air in our local market, they managed to draw a crowd around them with all sorts of visual aids, dressing-up and humour, before they shared the gospel with them. Among those who stopped and watched and listened were Diane and her older married sister Pauline.

Diane's view of church and Christians did not conform to what she observed there in the open air. She thought church was serious and boring and Christians were serious, boring people. These zany young people, not much different in age to herself, intrigued her. When they invited people to the Sunday morning meeting, she made up her mind to go along to find out more. This alarmed her older sister. Their mother had died a while before and Diane, very much younger than Pauline, still lived in the family home with her widowed father. Pauline was concerned that Diane was vulnerable and open to all sorts of harmful influences. She felt a motherly concern for her younger sister in the absence of mum, and knew nothing about The Salvation Army and what Salvationists believed and what they were like. Concerned that the Army might be some sort of manipulative sect, Pauline decided that she too would go to worship that Sunday morning with Diane. In fact, she told Janet, who was married to her husband's brother, about what had happened and she decided that she, too, would go.

And so it was that all three came to worship that Sunday morning and then the following Sunday morning, Easter morning, which was the cadets' last Sunday before returning to college. Diane continued coming for a few weeks, but the young people who had attracted her were no longer there and she gradually left off coming.

However, her sister Pauline, a mother of four, and Janet, a mother of three, continued to attend. Something deep within them had been stirred. They lived away from town in two villages that were not too far from one another, and so I offered to visit them both. They accepted. We would meet regularly in Pauline's home and they always had plenty of questions for me. Some were based on things that I had preached, some on things they had read in the Bible, the way of salvation, all sorts of questions. They told me how they were aware that many people at the corps had a *something* – something they couldn't describe but a definite *something* that they, too, wanted. They described it variously as a *serenity*, a *peace*, a *loveliness*, a *something*.

I explained what it is that happens inside people when they accept the truth about themselves as God sees it and they confess their sin to him (merely acknowledging what he already knows). With a definite desire to live to please him in future, they ask him for his mercy and forgiveness, on the basis that God's own Son Jesus Christ took on himself the punishment that they deserve to free them of the guilt and responsibility for their wrongdoing, sin. I described how a peace, and a sense of security and joy, will enter their hearts, the like of which they have never experienced before, and that this experience will sustain them through both the good times and the sad times, when life is all blessings and when life is all horror.

'And it's as easy to receive as that?' they asked.

'Yes, it's as easy as that,' I replied.

We prayed together. They prayed that God would forgive them and claimed Jesus Christ as their Saviour and Lord. I was really thrilled for them. We said our goodbyes as they rushed off to collect their children from school and I made my way home. However, next time we met together they were very downcast.

'We did all you said, but neither of us feel that we have what you have, that *something* we see in a lot of the other people in the church.'

'Just because you don't feel it doesn't mean that it isn't there,' I said.

'What do you mean?' one asked.

I then went on to explain that my mother and father lived more than 100 miles away. When we are on the telephone I feel assured of their love. On the days that I don't hear their voices I don't have that assurance, but does that mean anything has changed? Surely it is only my perception and feelings that are different. I shared with them the Scriptures, 'If we confess our sins, he is faithful and just and will forgive us our sins and purify us from all unrighteousness' [1 John 1:9] and, 'He who believes in the Son of God has the witness in himself' [1 John 5:10, *New King James Version*].

'Jesus now lives within you. I can see it. That witness to the truth is there. Even if you don't feel it, it doesn't mean it is not there. What you need, and need to pray for, is that God will give you that assurance that it is there, and he will. That *something* that you see in Christians is not something that they are always aware of, conscious of. In Exodus 34:29 when Moses came down the mountain with the two tablets of stone – the Ten Commandments – having spent a prolonged time in the presence of God, it says that his face shone. It shone with the glory of the Lord, but he was unaware of it. God will give you an assurance. It will be something that he gives you from time to time. The reason that he doesn't give you a permanent sense of his presence, his assurance, is that he wants you to take him at his word, not rest on your feelings.'

I prayed with them and I prayed when away from them. Was God withholding the blessing? Was it something they had withheld from him that prevented them from experiencing it? They were so earnest and so sincere and I, now their minister, didn't know what else to say or do. Each time we met, we had a lovely time and God blessed us all and we all learnt things, but that lack of assurance bugged them and it bugged me until one very special, quite unique Sunday.

Chapter 8

Eventual Harvest

On a Saturday night, as the shops were closing, I would make my way to the goods loading bay of a large store in town in a vehicle that had originally been a builder's van, which someone had converted into a caravanette for me. This was before the days of people carriers, but even had there been such things then I could never have afforded such a vehicle to transport our five children, my wife and me. Standard saloon cars were not big enough, and this converted van had not only seats, but beds, a sink and gas stove and all the mod cons necessary for us to be able, with the addition of a tent, to have holidays – albeit very basic ones. It also provided a means of transport for all sorts of other things, too, that were nothing to do with the family. It came in very useful for collecting and distributing food that had passed its sell-by date from this store, which I was now parked at the rear of.

About half an hour after the store closed, the vertical concertina metal shutters would clatter and crash open and trolleys would be wheeled out, piled high with large plastic trays loaded with fruit, vegetables, ready meals and other nutritious goodies. It wasn't an easy task trying to complete the weekly three-dimensional jigsaw puzzle that constituted loading my 'van'. I would then drive to the control centre of the local Careline, unload all the trays on to their car park and, with the aid of a list of my needy clients, reorganise their contents before reloading them on to my van, minus a few trays filled with food for the staff of Careline to distribute.

What or who was Careline? There were a large number of elderly people in our town, some in residential homes or sheltered accommodation, others still living independently in their own homes, who all had direct telephone access to and also an emergency button or string-pull contact with the centre, which was manned 24 hours a day. As well as help being available there 24 hours a day, mobile wardens would go out from the centre onto the district on a daily basis, visiting and checking on the welfare of their clients. When I met with the wardens to see whether they would help me by delivering food to those whom they knew were in particular need, they were thrilled to do it. They knew their clients better than I did and to have tried to distribute it all myself would have been a logistical nightmare. Having made my delivery at Careline, I would spend the next hour or two taking the rest of the trays round to poor families, families I knew or discovered to be genuinely struggling.

One of the difficulties of introducing oneself into a situation of need for the first time is that of doing so without causing embarrassment or offence. Most people have a degree of self-respect, self-esteem that might easily be threatened by an offer of help. A parent finding it hard to provide even the essentials for their family, secretly and irrationally questioning their capability, fitness or worthiness as a parent, could look on even a kindly offer of help, however humbly and sensitively made, as an indictment, a judgment of them.

On one occasion I was given an address on a housing estate where there was a family with five children, the youngest a baby. The husband was long-term unemployed and the mother had a hip problem that affected her walking. I found the house, parked and knocked at the door. I could hear the children's shrieks as they played together. I was sure they hadn't heard, so I knocked again. Eventually the mother came to the door. I introduced myself, told her where I was from, that I was passing by and just wondered whether she might appreciate some food to help with the family budget. Her name was Elizabeth.

'Would I? You bet!' she replied with a grin. 'Thank you very much.'

'If you can leave the door open I'll bring it straight through to the kitchen. Is that OK? I can let you have several trays, but I can't leave the trays with you, I have to take them back, so I would appreciate it if you could empty them.'

'Yes, I'll do that. Bring them straight through.'

On top of the first tray was a bunch of bananas, and as I entered the house a little chap wearing only a vest started jumping up and down excitedly and pointing, 'Bananas, bananas, bananas, Mummy!'

'Yes, I know they're bananas. Go and get some pants on and be a good boy and mummy might give you one,' Elizabeth responded.

Off the little one scampered. Dad came out into the kitchen. We introduced ourselves to one another and Keith helped me unload some more trays. We removed each item to the growing excitement of the children, who commented on every new discovery. They were all very grateful, shouting their thanks as I left. I felt a bit like Father Christmas.

And so my visits to Keith and Elizabeth's home became a regular feature of my Saturday nights and we got to know each other and built a friendship. From time to time they would ask me about what I was doing and I would take the opportunity of sharing what God was doing in various people's lives. Then one day Elizabeth asked if I 'did christenings'. I explained that in The Salvation Army we called it a dedication ceremony and that yes I did conduct dedication ceremonies. She then asked if I would conduct the dedication of their youngest, Steven. I said that I was willing but that I first needed them to understand what was entailed and the promises parents made on dedicating their child to God. We organised a day and time for me to visit and discuss the issue.

It was dark when I arrived and I was led into their one and only living room. The television was on with the children gathered round it.

'Oh, Mum,' they cried, as Elizabeth turned the volume down.

I then spoke of how a child is a gift from God – something with which both Keith and Elizabeth agreed – and that we, as Christians, believe that everyone that God creates is created with a purpose. I then went on to explain that believing that the best thing for a child was for it to grow up to know God and discover and fulfil that purpose a parent, or parents, promise to do all that they can to create an environment that would encourage this. I was aware that Keith was greatly distracted by the television and was only half attentive. Elizabeth, on the other hand, was totally attentive and somewhat embarrassed by Keith's head half turned to the television.

'Pay attention, Keith,' she kept saying.

'I am,' he kept on replying.

I ended by asking, 'If you believe that the best life for your children is a Christian life, lived in harmony with God, what about you? Why don't you consider it for yourselves? Why would you want it for your children and not yourselves if it's the best? It's something for you to think about.' We set a date for the dedication of Steven and I prayed and left.

Some weeks before the date that we had set, Elizabeth started to come to morning worship and it was not long after the dedication of Steven that she sought Christ as her Saviour. It transformed her. Despite her family and financial and physical struggles there was now a continuing air of joy in her that I hadn't seen before. It wasn't long after Steven's dedication that she informed me that there was another child on the way.

Soon after the birth of Jennifer, their next child, Elizabeth – now a soldier of the corps – asked if I could dedicate her. I agreed, but said that I would need to visit and go through what it was all about again with them. They had moved house. They now had a bigger home on a different estate. This time the children were out to play and Keith switched the television off when I entered the room. We shared together and I commented on the joy I had that Elizabeth had not only dedicated her child to God, but had dedicated herself, too. Keith was giving me undivided attention. In answer to a question I posed, Keith told me that Elizabeth's decision had changed her for the better. She giggled. Again at the conclusion of our time together I queried the anomaly of wanting the best for our children and yet not seeking it for ourselves. We had set a date for the ceremony, I prayed for the family and left.

One Sunday, a little while later, I mentioned to Rudi that we were dedicating Keith and Elizabeth's latest child the following Sunday morning.

'I know,' he said. He and Lesley had taken a particular interest in Keith and Elizabeth and were proving a great support to the family.

'Look, it might be my imagination but I think Keith has changed since the dedication of Steven. I don't think that he is far from Christ. I think the Lord is speaking to him. I have been praying much for them in recent weeks and I have something to request of you, Rudi.'

'What's that?' Rudi asked, inquisitively.

'Well, I don't know when it will be, but I know that you will recognise the moment. I really feel that it is you rather than me who is to do this. When you know the moment is right, and you *will* know, ask Keith, "Why don't you give your heart to Jesus Christ?" He will try to divert you by some humorous or sarcastic comment. Don't get distracted, just ask the question again, "Why don't you give your heart to Jesus?"'

Rudi had only been a Christian just over six months. This was all new to him. He looked somewhat bemused. 'Is that what you normally do?' he asked.

'No,' I replied. 'I've never done it that way in my life, but I believe that is what you are to do.'

'Oh,' he responded, with a wry smile. 'Well, I'm seeing Keith on Friday night. I take his oldest children home from youth club.'

'Don't jump the gun,' I quickly interrupted. 'Don't assume that it is this next week. It may be weeks, months or a year before you have to ask the question, but you will know it when you are to ask it and you will know that it is the right question to ask.'

I didn't see any of them again until Sunday morning. Keith and Elizabeth arrived for the meeting with their children. Other family members had also travelled to be there. I never realised until that morning that Keith had been brought up in a Christian home, or that his father was a Salvationist, but his father came up from London wearing his Salvation Army uniform. I was sad that the congregation was depleted, so many had gone away or decided to take what was a bank holiday Sunday off. I also discovered to my horror that there were insufficient personnel for the songsters to sing or the singing company (children's choir) or band to take part. My pianist was also away. Catastrophe – or so it seemed. On the one day that we were having so many visitors, too!

Halfway through the service I called the parents forward with baby Jennifer for the dedication ceremony and we completed that part of the service. Soon after that, one of the other children started to be disruptive. Elizabeth tried to control him, but he proved to be a handful. Keith took the child from her and walked up the aisle and out through the door, leaving the worship to stand out in the foyer. From where I stood, I could see him through the net curtains and large window at the rear of the hall, but although he could see what was going on I knew that he could not hear a word. I was so disappointed. Keith had only attended Sunday worship once before and that was when Steven was dedicated. After this visit he might well never set foot in the hall again. I had so hoped that he would hear God speaking to him that morning and respond. What hope had he of that now, I wondered?

I preached my heart out that morning, aware that Keith was watching but not hearing. I followed it with an appeal to respond to God, and Pauline, whose story I have already shared, left her seat and came and knelt at what we call the penitent form or mercy seat – our special meeting place with God, our special place of prayer. Then others came forward, some to rededicate themselves to God and others seeking him for the first time. I opened up the meeting for anyone in the congregation to pray and several people did. Then Keith's father, too, rose to his feet and prayed. I felt prompted, as he finished, to go and speak to him.

'Mr Goodall?'

He opened his eyes, 'Yes,' he said, and as he spoke I caught sight of Elizabeth, to my left, getting up and making her way into the aisle to go forward. 'Please can you go to Keith and take your grandson from him and just ask him to come in.' I paused, 'Tell him his wife has gone forward and that she has need of him.'

'OK,' he said and got up and left the hall.

There were two doors at the back of that hall, with an aisle leading from each to the front of the hall, with a large window between the doors. Keith didn't return through the doorway through which his father had left, instead he came in the other one. I was, therefore, standing in the wrong aisle when he entered. He stood there looking confused. I do not believe in misusing the things of God or manipulating people. I wondered what had made me say what I did. I now had to walk down the aisle, across the front and up the other aisle to greet Keith.

'Elizabeth has gone to the mercy seat and she needs you,' I said.

He went forward and knelt beside her. It was only then that I realised how true it was. Elizabeth and Keith loved each other, of that I had no doubt. Elizabeth had Keith on one level, but there was a deeper level on which she needed him. The mercy seat was now fully occupied with people who had come forward, each with someone counselling them and praying for them. I grabbed one chair then another from the empty front row and turned them round to make more space available should any more people wish to come forward and kneel before God.

As I placed one of the chairs in position, Keith rose to his feet and walked towards me with a very strange look on his face. I wondered what he was going to say, but as I waited for him to say something I was aware of someone approaching from my right side. Still holding the back of the chair in front of me, I turned and saw Rudi standing to my right looking quite sternly at Keith to my left. Rudi then lifted his hand and pointed his index finger first towards Keith and then down at the chair I was holding. Immediately they both dropped down on their knees. That morning Rudi led what was for him to be the first of many people to Christ.

I knew God was at work in that meeting although I did not know exactly what was happening. Servants often do not know what their master is doing, nor have they any right to. Their job is to fulfil their role, do what their master requires of them. Eleven people came forward that morning. Four came forward and received salvation; the other seven came forward to rededicate themselves to God.

Only after the service did I discover what had transpired between Rudi and Keith following my conversation with Rudi the previous

Sunday. He had indeed taken Keith's children home from youth club on the Friday as he said he would and, when they arrived at the house, Rudi ensured that the children made their way safely into the house. As he then leant down and fastened the gate, Keith wandered down the path towards him, hands in pockets with his shirt hanging out of his trousers. Rudi straightened up to discover that they were inches from each other, eyeball to eyeball.

'And I knew, just like you said that I would, that it was the moment,' Rudi told me. '"Keith," I said, "Why don't you give your heart to Jesus?"'

He chuckled back, ''Cause I haven't seen the light yet.'

'"Yes, you have," I responded. "Why don't you give your heart to Jesus?" I repeated. He just stood there, silent. We then said our goodbyes and I left. I knew that something was going on in him and while we were all praying this morning I was watching what was happening. When I saw Keith get up from the mercy seat I knew I had to go forward to talk to him.'

The meeting lasted two and a half hours, very long for us, but so wonderful, so Holy Spirit filled. As Pauline, the first to have come forward that morning, left the building, tears of joy were flowing from her eyes.

'I've found it, I've found it. At last I've found it!' she cried.

It was such a joy to share her joy. 'And where is your friend Janet today?' I asked.

'She's got the flu, she'll be so disappointed. I'm going straight round there before I go home to tell her. My hubby won't be happy. He'll wonder where I am. They've never had their dinner so late.'

I left the hall after the meeting, exhausted. I found it hard to eat my dinner. God had given us such a wonderful morning. 'How on earth could the evening meeting match that?' I thought. 'Keith, Elizabeth and their family and friends won't be there, it is always a smaller attendance in the evenings anyway, and on top of all that, so many people normally there are away with it being the Bank Holiday.'

I was aware of God's powerful presence even before the meeting began, and there, sitting with Pauline, was dear Janet, looking proper poorly. She should have been at home, tucked up in bed. Neither of them normally attended the evening meeting. I wondered what conversation had taken place between the two of them. The service was brief and, as we came to the end of the message and the appeal was given and prayer began, Janet came forward. Then over the next hour or so four others came forward to rededicate themselves to God. What appeared at first to have been a brief meeting extended to two hours before we sang the last song.

Janet was thick with flu. 'I had to come. I had to come. When Pauline told me what had happened to her I had to come, I so wanted it to happen to me.'

And it did. What a day. What an amazing day from our wonderful God who just loves giving his people surprises.

Chapter 9

The Hostel

It began with a battle in my soul.

Occasionally, very occasionally, I would go to the hostel for homeless men in our town with clothes I had been given for the needy. It was a derelict building, its furnishings were other people's throw-outs, most of its clientele were quite uncommunicative to any greeting and it had the most unpleasant smell. I had visited some of our older Salvation Army hostels in the past, but had never been in any as bad as this one, which was run by another organisation. I didn't like the place at all, yet a seed, unconsciously, was sown in my mind and there developed a growing feeling in me that I ought to be spending time in that place with those men who had shown very little interest in, never mind enthusiasm for, my company.

I had every argument and solid reason for not responding to the feeling, especially as no one else knew was going on within me. Like most officers in a busy corps, my weeks were full before they ever began. I argued internally for months. I avoided driving anywhere near the place, yet time and again I would see men around the town who were obviously from among its 42 male residents, and seeing them troubled me. I couldn't get the hostel out of my mind.

From experience I knew the difference between God's leadings and my ideas so, after months of inner turbulence and arguments, I surrendered and telephoned the hostel and asked the manager if it would be acceptable for me to come and visit the men on a regular basis. He asked me why I wanted to come and I replied that I did not really know!

'Do you want to preach to the men?'

'No,' I replied.

'Do you want to Bible-bash them?'

'No,' I again answered.

'Are you trying to get them into your church, then?'

Again I replied, 'No.'

'Then what is it that you want to come in here for?'

'Well, it may seem crazy to you, but for months now I've had this thing in me that won't go away, that I ought to be going into your hostel on a regular basis. I've battled against the idea. I've more than enough to do without trying to fit any more into my busy life, but this feeling – conviction – won't go away and I've come to the conclusion that God is speaking to me. Obviously I may be wrong. You may think that I'm a nutcase, but I believe that if it is God who wants me in your hostel, then he knows why and will no doubt reveal the reason to me when I get in there. My natural tendency is to have an agenda, a programme, a clear idea of what I am to say and do, and that's something I've had to fight in this case.'

I didn't know who the listener was or what he thought of my strange conversation. I wondered whether he thought I was some sort of 'religious nut', but he responded politely and told me that he would put it to the residents' committee and then ring me back with a decision afterwards. I would have to abide by what they agreed.

'Hooray,' I thought, 'I know that they won't want me!' (Isn't that terrible?)

A week later a telephone call brought the news to me that, while a third of the men on the committee definitely did not want me, the rest either didn't mind or thought it might be good. No one on the committee thought that me visiting would be of benefit to them personally (but remember they were all men!).

So the following Monday evening I went in. That hour's visit was awful. I felt so uncomfortable. I wandered from the pool room to the darts room to the television room and back again, like a ship unable to find an anchorage. No one responded to my feeble attempts to start conversation.

In the pool room I made some positive and encouraging remarks when one or other of the players potted a ball and was given a clear look of disapproval by them both. Half a dozen or more men were standing round the dartboard when I went into the darts room, having a darts tournament between themselves.

The moment I entered, one of them called out, 'We'd better watch our language, the vicar's here!' I do find bad language offensive, but I would prefer people to be honest, to be themselves, rather than have to put on a show because I am with them. I would rather the bad language stop because the person using it no longer desires to speak in that way than because I am there. After all, it was their home and I was merely a visitor in their home.

As for the television room, the lights were off and men sat in silence, glued to the brightly coloured screen. It was a long hour. I couldn't wait to get out of the building. The end couldn't come soon enough. I left relieved that it was over, determined that that was that and that I would not be returning. I thought what a stupid idea of mine it had all been. Yet, as I stepped out into the cool of the evening, I somehow knew it was where I ought to be and that I had to go back the following Monday.

I returned the following week. Again I wandered seemingly aimlessly between the various recreation rooms unable to start conversation with anyone. Somewhat disheartened, I gave up and went and slouched in a vacant chair in the television lounge where a group of about a dozen men were sat in the dark. They were watching the James Bond film *Octopussy*. Silence reigned in the room.

I thought to myself, 'What a waste of time. If I had wanted to watch television, I could have stayed at home and enjoyed the company of my family.' Then, following a ridiculously far-fetched incident on the screen, I expressed out loud an observation that resulted in the whole room erupting in laughter. I didn't think that what I had said was that funny, but the men obviously did. For the rest of the film the silence was gone as the audience ridiculed the film scene by scene with tremendous humour.

When it was over someone switched the television off and another switched the lights on and it seemed that all eyes were on me. Tongue in cheek, I just said, 'You are all younger than me,' (well they were a little). 'When I was a boy we had a big telly with a very small screen and every night there were cowboy films, all in black and white, no colour in those days – *Wells Fargo, Rawhide…*'

Now, most of the men were in their 40s and weren't *that* much younger than me, and it seemed that I had pressed a button in each of their heads, albeit inadvertently, for they quickly added to the list that I had begun, shouting out, *Wagon Train! Man From Laramie! Maverick! Bonanza!* (For those readers too young to recognise these titles, they are all cowboy programmes of the 1960s). The list seemed endless. The ice had broken but my hour had long passed. Like Cinderella at the ball when the clock struck midnight I suddenly realised that I should be elsewhere. I was already late for another appointment and so I had to say a speedy goodbye and leave. But as I hurried down the corridor towards the exit, I heard the words 'See you next week' echoing from several voices behind me.

As I arrived the third week, a man asked if he could have a private word with me. We went off into the grounds and sat in the sun on some broken furniture that had been left there. He shared his story, entrusting me with much that was very personal, things that he had never shared with anyone. After a while, other residents who spotted us there were curious to know what we were talking about and, one by one, they strolled over towards where we were sitting.

Obviously we had to change the conversation from a private to a more general one. Eventually there were ten or more of these men standing around us or, like us, sitting on the broken furniture. They started to join in. Everything was light and humorous. One man with brilliant white hair and an equally brilliant white moustache, whose name – so I was later to discover – was Mo, started to speak detrimentally about me and people like me who call themselves Christians, telling me we were all hypocrites. Knowing he didn't know me I asked him how he'd found out. He didn't answer the question, but told me that he was better than a 'load of the so-called Christians who go to church'.

'I should hope so,' I replied.

'What do you mean?' he asked, looking confused.

'Well, it's the worst people who go to church. They go to church because they know they are bad and that they need forgiveness. Good people like you obviously don't need forgiveness. People who are well don't need a doctor. Doctors are for sick people. Church is for bad people.' Then I added, tongue in cheek, 'And the worst lot go to The Salvation Army, but don't tell them I told you so. I should know, I'm one of them!' There were guffaws of laughter at this, but I could tell that a number of the guys were thinking.

'Why would anyone want to belong to a church that isn't what it ought to be?' someone asked. I agreed that the Church had failed and that I would like to say that my part of it was different, but that it, too, was not all it ought to be or that God would have it be, and that I didn't know a church that was. I then explained that, on becoming a Christian, I had decided to make God the governor of my life and to do what he wants rather than what I want and that, as a result, I had become the happiest man in the world. I was in The Salvation Army simply because I was thoroughly convinced that it was where God desired me to be, not because it was the best thing since sliced bread. And never mind the church, despite my years of walking with Jesus I was still not what he wanted *me* to be. I hope I am not what I once was and today I am a better man than I was yesterday, but I am still not what I ought to be.

'I bet you wouldn't want the likes of us in your church, mate,' said one man.

'Oh yes, I would,' I replied, 'I would love you all to come. The church needs to change. If I could, I'd even pay all 42 of you guys who live in this place to come to our place of worship every week and just sit yourselves down in the middle of our hall. It would do us the world of good to have you there. We would have to change, we would have to adapt. In fact we need you more than you need us!'

They then asked how I could believe in a God of love with so many innocents suffering in the world. I told them of some of our family's personal tragedies which have baffled me, but how I know from experience that God is good, that a person can know God well enough to be able to trust him with what he cannot understand and does not know, and that one day when I get 'home' he will explain it all to me. Mo then asked me how I could believe in someone that I couldn't see and, as I opened my mouth to reply, another man, big and burly, with large earrings and closely cropped hair – a hard nut and no mistake – butted in. His language was bad, expletives every other word, yet beyond the surly manner and offensive language I heard something deeper.

'What did you used to do in the Navy, Mo?' the man asked.

'You know what I used to do,' replied Mo.

'I do, but he don't,' the man responded, pointing at me.

'Nor do we,' a few others added.

'I used to work in the engine room of the aircraft carrier *Ark Royal*,' Mo said.

'Didn't you ever worry about crashing? Hitting rocks or another ship or the harbour at speed?' the man asked him.

''Course I didn't,' Mo responded.

'Why not?' the big man asked.

''Cause the captain was in control on the bridge!' was the reply.

'How did you know, you couldn't see the bridge.'

I just sat there mesmerised at what was going on and looking from one to the other as though I was a spectator at Wimbledon.

'Well, they would never leave the bridge unmanned,' Mo answered.

'Yeah, but how did you know?'

'It was a rule, it was never to be left with no one on lookout,' said Mo.

'It may have been a rule, but how could you be sure? How did you know that the rule wasn't being broken?'

'Well, they would never do that. They would never leave the bridge unmanned.' Mo was now getting agitated.

The big guy just kept coming back with the same question, plus expletives, 'How did you know?'

Eventually Mo, weak from repeating himself, wearily bleated, 'I just knew that someone would be there looking after it all!'

'You had faif, Mo, faif in what you couldn't see!' the big man shouted aloud in his strong south-London accent.

I was taken aback. In response to these words, Mo asked me another question. I responded by asking the big man his name.

'Geoff!' he replied, in a manner and with a look that seemed to threaten. 'And what business is that of yours?'

'Mo's question is in response to what you said, Geoff, so why don't you answer him?' Geoff did.

Again, responding to Geoff's second answer, Mo asked me a third question. Geoff would have denied it, his language and attitude disguised it, but I thought, 'God has been speaking to you and you've heard.' So I turned again to Geoff and said, 'I pray every day, read the Bible every day, preach every week, but you're far better at this than I am, Geoff. We ought to change places. Do you want to answer him?'

This was greeted by hoots of raucous laughter. I was bemused. I didn't know Geoff, or why the idea of us changing places was so funny. I didn't know what they all knew, that Geoff was an alcoholic and that the picture that I had given, of him on a Salvation Army platform or in a church pulpit and me, highly inebriated, doing some of the things that Geoff did, was really comical. Again, as Geoff spoke, I could hear an echo of God's word and wisdom despite Geoff's bad language. More than an hour had passed and I had to leave.

Sunday evening came and, as I mounted the platform and looked across the congregation, there in the middle of the hall sat Geoff and another man from the hostel, Alan. I could not help wondering what had brought them to worship that evening. I had made a point of not inviting the men at the hostel to our services, not because I did not want them there – quite the contrary – but rather because I did not want any of them to get the impression that I was visiting them to get them into my church. I wanted them to realise that my sole reason and motive was concern for them.

The service ended and we shook hands at the door and they left. They were there again the following Sunday night, but each Monday evening, when I visited the hostel, neither they nor I mentioned their visits to the corps.

I now looked forward very much to my weekly visit to my new-found friends. Some self-contained flats had been built at the back of the hostel and one Friday, when I popped by with a bag of used clothes to hand in at the reception, Geoff saw me and invited me for coffee in his new home. My dinner was waiting for me at home, I was hungry and my wife was expecting me, but I accepted the invitation, knowing my wife would understand what I was about.

Geoff proudly showed me his brand new flat. He was one of the residents chosen to move out of the institutional setting and communal living of the hostel to have a proper tenancy of one of these self-contained flats. The plan was for him to take on personal responsibility for himself, with continuing support of an appointed hostel key worker to help him and monitor his progress. Tenancy of one of these flats would be a resident's first step into returning to society.

The flat consisted of an open kitchen/lounge area. The kitchen had a cooker, fridge, sink and modern oak-finish units and the lounge area had a sofa, an armchair, a dining table with two chairs and some shelves on a wall. There was a separate bedroom and shower/WC room. All the furnishings were new and the flat was cosy and full of light.

While we sat at the table, sharing together, Geoff spoke of the conversation and banter I had had with the men sitting out in the evening sunshine on broken furniture, some weeks earlier. The memory of that evening and Geoff's words at the time were firmly etched in my mind.

He then told me how he had overslept and got up late the following morning and that had he not done so, what then followed would never have happened. I was intrigued at what he went on to say. He explained how, when he awoke, he had sat thinking about all that had been shared the night before and had then gone downstairs to the darts room and found an old Bible – or rather half a Bible. It had been a handy missile on several occasions when fights broke out, like several of the other tatty books that sat on a shelf in that room.

Taking it back to his bed he sat down and the Bible fell open at Matthew's Gospel. He began reading where it opened, chapter 5, the Sermon on the Mount. Eventually reaching chapter 7 verse 7, he stopped when he read the words, 'Ask, and it shall be given you; seek, and ye shall find; knock, and it shall be opened unto you.'

'I asked myself,' said Geoff, '"Do I believe that?" And then thought to myself, "Yes, I do." Then the question came into my head, "So what are you going to do about it?" I just knelt down at my bedside and asked God to forgive me for the great mess that I had made of my life, all that I had done wrong, and to come into my life and change me. I was down there a long time and when I got up I didn't feel any different, like I thought I might, but I knew that I was different.'

I was stunned, absolutely elated, but stunned. I should have guessed, but it never dawned on me what had happened, even though he had changed and had been behaving very differently to the Geoff I met that first night. Never mind the fact that, uninvited, he had started to come to worship, his language had been so different since that night. Instead of his sentences being punctuated by expletives every other word, such words rarely left his lips. Yet for some reason I had hardly noticed until what he shared with me woke me up. He then went on to tell me of all the blessings and apparent coincidences and amazing things he had experienced in the two weeks that had followed.

'I feel so high and it's cost me no money and I don't have a hangover in the morning like I did with drink or drugs,' he said. Then, getting very emotional, he told me how he felt he ought to be doing something in response to the wonderful thing God had done for him. I thought for a moment.

'I have an idea,' I said, 'but give it some thought and prayer, Geoff. Vicar-types like me are often full of ideas for other people that are not always God's ideas.'

'What's that?' he asked.

'I would love you to tell the congregation all that you have shared with me. Christians often do believe what God can do – in theory. They accept what he did in the Bible, but somehow don't believe that he can do the same today. They fail to connect the two, the God of the Bible and the God of today. They don't realise that he hasn't changed.'

'I'll do that,' was his rapid response.

'You don't need to make an immediate decision, go away and think about it, pray about it. Don't say "yes" unless you are certain, because once you do I'll rip your arm off! I won't let you reverse it.'

'No, I'm sure it's what I ought to do,' he laughed. 'When would you like me to do it?'

'This Sunday, the day after tomorrow,' I replied.

'What?'

'I warned you!'

Geoff laughed out loud again, 'No, that will be OK.'

Chapter 10

Never Too Old

A 70-year-old widow joined our over-60 club. Having moved to our town from Essex to be nearer to one of her daughters, Joan decided that she needed to make an effort to make a new life for herself. She joined several social groups in town, including our club. As a result of coming to our club and meeting some of the members of the church there, she began attending Sunday morning worship.

A few weeks passed and my wife and I went to visit her in her upstairs flat, part of a semi-detached dwelling. A really pleasant woman, she told us something of her life story. She was a Christian and she had gone to church prior to her move. She had been diagnosed with Parkinson's Disease a few years earlier and it was slowly progressing.

Only during subsequent visits did we discover the nature of her previous 'church'. It was a spiritualist 'church'! We discovered that, alongside her 'faith' in Jesus, she was a spiritualist who took part in seances, which she apparently began to attend when she was grieving after the loss of her husband.

Following a lot of heart-searching and prayer I decided that, for the time being, I would leave the subject of her spiritualism to one side and concentrate our conversations on Jesus. As Joan became more involved in the corps her focus and attention on Jesus grew, she really came alive in Christ and she testified to the fact that she now had a deep personal relationship with him.

For a while, in the early days, she had openly mentioned her spiritualist leanings and involvement to some of the congregation. These conversations were reported back to me with a demand by some that I speak to her about her views, as they were not the views of a true

Christian and were at odds with the Bible's explicit teaching. It was definitely an issue that needed dealing with, but I wanted to ensure that she was firmly committed to Christ before I pulled her false props away.

My wife and I visited Joan some time later and she told us how she had changed so much since linking up with us and how she felt the Lord wanting her to become a soldier (enter full membership). Knowing that we now had a good relationship, I shared with her what the Bible had to say about the occult and spiritualism and discovered that it was no longer an important issue. She had developed her own doubts and, in fact, had not been involved in it for quite some length of time.

As we prayed together she relinquished all connections with what had, at one time, been so important to her. In addition she said that she really wanted to do more, to be more committed in a practical way.

'But what can an old wrinkly of 70 with Parkinson's do?' she asked.

Seventy she may have been but, amazingly, wrinkly she was not. I shared with her my conviction that everyone is equally important before God, that we all have a role to fulfil that is our role and no one else's, whoever we are, and that each of our roles is essential to the wellbeing and effective functioning of the whole body, the Church. Judy and I then assured her that we would pray, and suggested that she should pray that God himself would make clear what he had in mind for her to do.

So the prayers for that area of Joan's life began. She may have been 70 and have limited mobility, but she was a lighthouse of optimism and joy in the corps and a positive encouragement to all she met. It seemed only natural that, after a period of discipling, Joan should be accepted into full soldiership within the corps. Yet, despite months of faithful prayer, she and we were still seeking God's particular role for her.

On the Sunday following my Friday night chat with Geoff in his new flat, Geoff turned up for morning worship for the first time, this time on his own. With her worsening condition and mobility problems, it took a considerable amount of energy and effort for Joan to attend worship, so she only ever attended the one meeting on a Sunday, and that was the one in the morning. Geoff sat in the centre block of seats not far from the front of the hall, while Joan sat to one side some rows further back.

At the end of worship, my wife and I left the worship hall and went and stood by the main door to the building to shake hands with exiting worshippers. I wandered out of the door into the sunshine talking with one of them and, finishing conversation, turned to face the door as Joan came out. She was short and thin with a walking stick and a beaming smile. She moved off to my left as Geoff, immediately behind her, shook my hand and proceeded to follow her.

'Hey, where are you going, Geoff? You live in that direction,' I jokingly called, pointing with my finger.

He turned round to face me. 'I'm going round Joan's for coffee!' he laughed.

As he turned to catch up with Joan, she must have heard him say her name for she turned round and her eyes met mine. Immediately I realised that God had answered our prayers. This was to be her ministry – encouragement, hospitality. I put my two thumbs up and mouthed a big 'yes' to her, and she, half turned, put up her thumb with the hand that was free.

Geoff saw her gesture and immediately looked round to me to see who Joan was signalling to. I still had my two thumbs in the air. He obviously did not know what all this was about and I must have looked suspicious and foolish as I tried to quickly hide my thumbs by rapidly plunging my hands into my pockets. In fact, I later discovered that he thought that there was some sort of conspiracy between Joan and me but, as he spoke with Joan over their coffee together, logic told him there could not have been. He had never heard of Joan and Joan had never heard of him. They attended different services and no one knew that Geoff was going to come along to morning worship for the first time that morning.

Also, as they talked together, Joan discovered that despite saying 'yes' to my suggestion that he tell the congregation that evening about what Jesus had done in his life, the sight of so many people in the Sunday morning meeting, and the reality of what lay before him in the evening, had totally unnerved Geoff. So Joan was able to reassure him and encourage him that all would be well, adding that Satan was wanting to stop him glorifying Christ Jesus. She then said that, normally, she only ventured out once on a Sunday because of her condition but, if it would help and if Geoff would come and accompany her to the hall, she would love to go and support him.

It was a few weeks later, in conversation with Joan, that I discovered exactly what happened as worship drew to a close that Sunday morning. She had noticed the back of this rather big chap with earrings sitting in the middle of the centre block of chairs and felt a compulsion to go and speak to him, even though she had never met him before and knew nothing about him. She explained how she didn't feel that she walked to him but that she 'just floated to him'! Geoff was 46 years of age, a big guy covered in tattoos, a hard-living boozer and bruiser when I had met him a few weeks earlier. His answer to problems was his two fists and he was an alcoholic of 25 years' standing to boot. What a courageous woman Joan was.

That night, when I climbed the platform and looked out on the congregation, there were Geoff and his friend Alan, who had been with him each of the preceding Sunday evenings, plus a third big guy from the hostel, Fred, Geoff's best pal – also an alcoholic – with petite little Joan sitting in the middle. The sight tickled me; it reminded me of the film image of a matriarchal mafia family, mama with her boys! I was also intrigued to see Fred there too, and later discovered that the reason that Fred came was twofold. Firstly, he could not believe the change in Geoff, or some of the things that he had witnessed himself while with Geoff during the previous few weeks. Secondly, he could not believe that any church would allow such a man as Geoff to stand in a pulpit and speak.

Geoff's testimony had a profound effect on the congregation that night as he stood there and showed them the half-Bible that he had found in the darts room that Tuesday morning and shared all that had transpired since reading it. Because of his drinking, his marriage had been destroyed. He had effectively lost his wife and three children. Drink had ruined his life and the lives of those he loved.

As we reached the end of the meeting, I announced the final song and everyone stood and sang their hearts out – all, that is, except Fred, Geoff's friend. I watched. He stood motionless and silent then, on the very last verse, he turned and walked out of the hall.

'Why?' I wondered.

*   *   *

It's now 11 years since Geoff last touched drink. So extraordinary was the change in his life that a number of the hostel staff and residents came to his enrolment as a uniformed soldier. He went on to minister to prisoners at one of our local prisons for several years. Subsequently, he met and married a lovely Christian woman and moved to another town nearby for a few years, before moving out of the area entirely. Whenever I think of him or speak with him, I still get deeply moved. I still find it hard to believe he's the same man as the one I first met. I guess that's because he isn't.

Joan maintained an open house for the men who came along to our corps from the hostel, even though her health continued to deteriorate. Walking became more and more difficult and she eventually became dependent on an electric scooter. Her wonderful ministry only terminated when she was forced to go into a residential home. Even there she was a lighthouse for the Lord to both staff and residents until the Lord finally came and took her to be with him. Despite her suffering and difficulties, her faith never wavered and even now her godly influence in the lives of so many men lives on.

Chapter 11

Sought And Found

Fred left the service while the last song was being sung – while the very last verse of the last song was being sung to be precise – and I was baffled. The meeting was almost over, why would he suddenly want to leave so near the end? I couldn't wait to deliver the benediction and follow him to find out. On the word 'Amen', I hurried from the platform, down the corridor and out of the front door, leaving my wife to shake hands with the departing congregation. I could see Fred some way down the street illuminated by the light shining from the lamppost where he had paused to light a cigarette. I ran down to him. Fred was another big, burly man, just like Geoff.

'Are you OK, Fred?' I asked.

'No I'm not, Captain. Look at me, I'm shaking.'

Indeed, he was shaking.

'What happened Fred?' I asked.

'Something odd happened in there,' he replied. 'I was frozen to the spot. I knew I had to go forward or get out, so I got out.'

'Wrong move, Fred,' I responded. Not wanting him to be embarrassed, I asked if he would like me to pop by and see him on my way back from my prison-visiting the following day. He said that he would.

Like Geoff, Fred was one of the hostel residents who had been allocated one of the new flats. When he opened his door the following afternoon he was still visibly upset. I was hardly in the door when he started talking about the previous evening.

'Wow, I don't know what happened last night,' he said. 'Look, I'm still shaking! When I got in last night I just broke down and cried like a baby. I haven't cried since I was a boy. I couldn't stop. A couple of mates knocked on my door and I couldn't stop crying and daren't unlock the door and face them. I've never been like this. I don't understand it.'

'I do, mate,' I replied. 'Last night you met with God. He loves you and he's been seeking you for years.' I then explained how much God loved him and what God had done in Jesus; that what he had done for Geoff he wanted to do for him.

'You heard God, Fred. You didn't respond to him, you ran off in the opposite direction, but you did hear him.' Fred then allowed me pray with him.

On leaving his flat, as I shook his hand and was about to depart, I just added, 'I also want to tell you Fred, that wherever you go, whatever you do, whether or not we ever meet again or you ever come to one of our meetings again, you will never, ever forget what you experienced last night.'

Fred came every Sunday evening for the next three months. He even spent Boxing Day with my wife and family in our home together, with a few of the other men from the hostel. We had great fun, but he just would not let go and surrender his life to Jesus.

After Christmas he stopped attending worship and a few months later he left the hostel and moved out of town. On very rare occasions we would bump into each other and chat a little – that is, if he was on his own. Sometimes, if he was with friends and I called his name he would act as if he didn't know who I was. That hurt.

I hadn't seen Fred for a year when I was visiting one of our people, Harry, a recently widowed man who was blind and housebound. As we shared together there was a knock at the door. It was Harry's neighbour, a retired gentleman who had been to the supermarket to do his shopping. Harry introduced Bob to me, telling me what a wonderful neighbour he was. When I heard the surname (not a common one), I asked him if he was related to a Fred with the same surname.

'That's my brother!' he exclaimed.

'Well I never,' I replied. 'I used to visit him in the local hostel and he did come to our services for a while, but I haven't seen him for about a year now. I do worry about him and he's always in my prayers.'

'Oh, that Fred. That's my brother's son, my nephew. I worry about him too. He's been a heartache,' said Bob. After further conversation he left. I never met him again or had contact until, about six months later, out of the blue, he phoned me.

'Hi there, Captain. I've got Fred here, he's very upset and in a terrible state. I don't know what to do. I told him that I had met you and he says that you are the only one that he's willing to see and to talk to.'

I was hoping to have an evening at home with my family, but needs must.

'Tell him I will be with him soon. Where is his flat? I can come to his flat and have coffee with him there.' I could hear Bob checking out my suggestion with Fred in the background.

Bob then spoke again, 'Fred says that you can't go round to his flat.'

He didn't need to tell me why. 'OK, I'll be with you in ten minutes and we'll decide what to do and where to go when we meet.' I drove to Bob's flat and met Bob and his wife. Fred came out and got into the car.

'I feel terrible, Captain, bothering you like this when I've had nothing to do with you for so long.'

'Don't worry about that. I'm your friend. That's what friends are for. Shall we pop into town and get a coffee?'

'I'd rather you didn't. I'm sorry to say that I've been taking drugs as well as the drink and there are people that know me there. I might bump into a "pusher".'

'What about ....?' I suggested another town a few miles away. 'There's a coffee shop in the Tesco store there, how about that? Does anyone know you in that town?'

'Yes, there are some, but not as many. That will be OK,' he replied. We talked as I drove and Fred told me about all that had happened since last we had seen each other. It was a catalogue of dreams dashed, promises broken, hopes unfulfilled. We spent a couple of hours over our coffee and at the end of our time there, before I offered to pray, I asked him one more question.

'Fred, it's nearly three years since you first came along to the Army. I just want to ask you one self-indulgent question, if I may?'

'Go ahead,' he replied.

'Do you ever think of what happened to you the first time that you came to one of our meetings?'

'All the time,' he replied. 'It's always on my mind. It haunts me,' he said, with a hurt look in his eyes. I just smiled and then he added, 'I know… I know what I've got to do.' I made no further comment. After praying for him we left and I drove him back to his flat.

'Look, Fred,' I said as he went to get out of the car, 'please keep in touch. I care about you. Even if you never come near our place again, please don't cut yourself off from me.' He assured me that he wouldn't, that he valued our friendship and that he was sorry for the way he had treated me.

'No problem,' I replied, before again asking God's blessing upon him. We parted and I went home. I heard nothing more from Fred. After quite some months, I did telephone his Uncle Bob to see if he knew how he was, as Fred's flat was not far from his.

'He was evicted a few months ago. I've no idea where he is now,' Bob told me.

A year or more then passed with no contact. Then one Friday afternoon, as I was leaving the house for a meeting, the telephone rang.

'I've just seen Fred. He's lost his flat, he's sleeping rough and he looks terrible!' It was Richard, another man from the hostel who had got saved and was now part of our corps. I couldn't respond immediately, there were 70 people waiting for me at the hall.

'Tell him I'll be with him in about 90 minutes,' I said. 'I can't come straight away. Tell him to wait and I'll be there.'

As soon as the meeting ended I rushed from the hall to the shopping precinct from where Richard had telephoned me. Neither Fred nor Richard was there. I scoured the town looking for Fred, to no avail. I phoned Richard who told me that Fred was not prepared to wait for me.

Just a week or so later, I got a message to say that Fred had cut his wrists the previous night and had been rushed into hospital. I felt terrible for not having got to him. I telephoned the hospital the following day with the intention of visiting him with my wife, only to discover that he had been discharged.

When I asked the sister where he had been discharged to, she replied, 'Home.'

'But he doesn't have a home. He has been sleeping rough down the marshes,' I responded. I searched the town to find him, all to no avail. The hospital was ten miles away. He had little cause to come back to our town. Few people really cared about him and all his family, except Bob, had given up on him. I wanted to make contact but had no idea where he might be. All I could do was to take my concern to God in prayer and ask others to pray for Fred too.

Then, four days later, on my homeward journey following a morning spent with prisoners in a prison some miles from our town, I felt an inner urge to go and find him.

Wondering whether this sudden compulsion, conviction, was from God, and with no one else in the car, I prayed aloud, 'Lord, if this is you, you know where Fred is. I do not have the remotest idea where to start looking for him. If you want me to find him, you will have to guide me, you will have to find him for me.'

God gave me no finger in the sky to follow, no supernatural sign. I just drove into the town instead of going home for a midday snack. I randomly (or so it seemed) selected a car park to head for, with no sense of God responding to my cry.

It was as I drove past the police station, the library and the post office towards the war memorial that I spotted Fred, with his head down in his hands, sitting on one of the seats that surround it. In fact, had I not followed the bend of the road to enter the car park and kept driving in a straight line, I would have mounted the pavement and hit him! I was amazed. I still am after all these years, for I am convinced that, despite my lack of any consciousness of the fact, God led me to Fred that day. I really didn't need to look for him.

Having parked the car, I wandered over to where Fred was and sat down beside him. He didn't look up or acknowledge my presence. His eyes remained transfixed on the pavement, his mind lost in his own world, unaware of my company.

'Hello, Fred.'

He was dirty, unkempt and unshaven. He looked up and at the sight of me said something that made it clear that he wanted me to go away. I responded to his hostility by saying that I was his friend and would not go away. He then told me that he didn't want to live and that he had tried to take his life.

'I know,' I replied.

'Who told you?' he snarled.

'Never mind that. Was it a serious attempt or a cry for help?' I asked.

'It was serious,' he responded, showing me how there are two alternative ways to cut one's wrist and the one that is chosen depends on what one intends to do.

'So what happened?' I asked.

'What do you mean, what happened?'

'Well, you tried to take your life, but you're still here,' I responded.

'The knife was too blunt and I was too drunk,' he replied. Silence followed. I didn't know what to say or do.

'When did you last have a drink?' I asked.

'Two days ago. I don't have any money. If I had money I would be drunk now.'

'When did you last eat?'

'I don't remember,' he replied.

Again, silence reigned. Then a thought entered my mind as to what to say next. It didn't fit my view of what a Christian should say to such a poor soul in such a situation, but somehow I had to break through this wall that surrounded Fred. I waited with bated breath and then blurted out, 'You're a complete failure aren't you, Fred?' The words coming out of my lips shocked me when I heard them and they shocked Fred. He looked up startled and angry.

'What do you mean?' he snorted.

'Well, you can't even take your own life.'

'You sod!' he exclaimed. Not language I like to hear or I ever use, but it seemed right on this occasion to accept the defamatory description that Fred gave me.

'Maybe so, but I'm a sod that loves you and what other one is here for you today.' The spell was broken. Fred now made eye contact and a smile grew across his face.

'My car's over there, let's get you something to eat and check out the hostel,' I suggested.

'No, Captain. I stink, I can't face anyone and I definitely can't get into your car.'

'You do stink, but get in the car, Fred,' I responded, trying to lighten things. Reluctantly, a very wobbly Fred walked to the car park.

'I think I'm suffering from malnutrition,' he said. I managed to coax him to accept a bag of chips, and I then suggested that he come and share in a meal that we were having at the hall that very evening. We were running an Alpha course and a meal was an integral part of the evening.

He declined, embarrassed at his state of dress and cleanliness. I told him that there would be one or two people at the hall who would remember him and be pleased to see him whatever his state, and that my wife would be disappointed that he didn't want to eat what she was cooking. It happened to be her turn on the rota, and he had often complimented her on the meals she had provided when he came to our home all those years earlier. I then suggested that I take him to the hostel where we had first met.

There were no members of staff available to conduct the interview when we got to the hostel, and I could tell by the way that Fred conducted himself that all the confidence he had once shown was gone. We were asked to return in two hours and we agreed to go back.

I then took him down to our hall where a women's meeting was taking place. He didn't want to be seen, so I ushered him into a side room and told my wife, who was helping in the kitchen. She took him a cup of tea and spent some time talking to him. He then went into the toilet to wash himself and freshen himself up a bit.

71

Meanwhile, I telephoned Geoff's house and left a message with his wife. It was by then four years since Geoff had last touched a drop of drink after 25 years of addiction. When Geoff got home he returned my call.

'I'm coming over,' he said in response to what I told him had happened to his old buddy, Fred. Geoff, now married to a lovely Christian woman, lived more than 13 miles away in another town.

'You can't drive, Geoff. Your wife told me about the operation you had on your hand yesterday and that you have only been home a few hours. I was only telephoning to get you to pray that God might do something while Fred is with us,' I told him. 'By the way, why didn't you tell me about your op?'

'Didn't want to bother you. Look, I'll catch the bus, I've got to come,' he replied. I sensed his concern for Fred in his voice. 'Anyway, my hand isn't the only reason I can't drive across. The wife crashed the car yesterday!'

I took Fred for his interview at the hostel. He's a big man, but he wanted me in the room with him. He was frightened of being rejected, having well and truly blotted his copybook when he left the hostel years before. It was obvious, despite the pleasant way that we were received, that Fred would not be going back there.

We then left the hostel, and I gave Fred a lift back into the town centre. 'Be at the hall at 7.20 pm, Fred,' I said as we parted.

'I'll be there,' Fred answered, as he got out of the car.

Geoff, his hand heavily strapped up, was already at the hall when I arrived an hour before the meal was to be served.

'Where's Fred?' he asked.

'I told him to come in an hour's time. We can go and find him if you like,' I suggested.

'Do you know where he is, then?'

'No,' I responded.

'Then how will you know where to find him?' Geoff queried.

'Well, God's found him once today, I am sure that he can do it again,' I quipped. Sure enough, as we drove down our one-way high street and reached the parish church, there was Fred sitting on the bench by the church wall, enjoying the early evening sunshine of what had been a sunny May day. I pulled the car over, got out and went over to him. When he saw me approaching, his first thought must have been that I had come to find him because I didn't believe he would turn up on his own.

'I *am* coming. You told me 7.20 pm,' he said, a little distressed.

'I know, don't worry about that. I've got a surprise for you, Fred, that's why I've come to find you. Jump in the car.' As Fred climbed into the back seat of the car and Geoff turned round to greet him, there was something electric in their encounter, a deep, emotional stirring that I know all three of us felt.

When I had met them more than four years earlier, both men had been in a very low state, both had had a tendency to violence and abuse. Since last they met, each had travelled a long way, but in totally opposite directions.

We arrived at the hall, and I left Geoff and Fred in a small room to talk together. After half an hour or so, they joined the other people who had arrived for the meal. One man at the meal, who knew Geoff and Fred from his days in the hostel, was so disturbed at the state of Fred that he walked home and brought back some of his own clothes for him.

After the meal I told Fred that he could leave, but he said that he didn't want to leave, that he wanted to see the video presentation that was to follow. Again, I tried to persuade him, telling him that I hadn't given him the meal to make him feel guilty or obliged to stay for the evening. Again, he insisted that he did want to stay and watch the film.

Among everything else in that evening's video presentation, Nicky Gumbell spoke on a verse from Revelation (3:20): 'Here I am! I stand at the door and knock. If anyone hears my voice and opens the door, I will come in and eat with him, and he with me,' illustrating it with a picture of Holman Hunt's painting of *The Light Of The World* which hangs in St Paul's Cathedral.

He described how the painting depicts Jesus standing at a door that is overgrown with ivy and weeds and how the door represents the door of someone's life. This person has never allowed Jesus into his or her life. Jesus is standing at the door knocking, awaiting a response. He wants to be a part of that person's life. Apparently someone commented to Holman Hunt that he had made a mistake and forgotten to paint the handle on the door, to which Holman Hunt replied, 'Oh no, that is deliberate. There is only one handle and that is on the inside.'

I was in the kitchen washing the dishes, pots and pans, oblivious to the video's content that evening, and the others watching the presentation were oblivious to the effect of that word on Fred. When he was quite a young boy, a church minister or priest had visited his school and given each child a copy of that very picture and told them exactly the same thing, that there is only one handle on the door of the human heart and that it is on the inside. Christ does not force his way in, he has to be invited into our lives. The memories of that lesson long ago all came flooding back to Fred that evening.

The presentation over, the audience separated into two groups to discuss what they had seen and Fred and Geoff went into the main worship hall to talk again. I was still ploughing through the washing and wiping up when Geoff came in and said, 'Please can you take over, Captain, I can't take things any further.' I obviously had no idea of what had been said up to this point, but as I entered the worship hall I felt the power of God's presence in the room and the thought entered my head, 'If only Fred wants to have Jesus in his heart.' I went and sat on one side of Fred, Geoff was on the other.

'How are you, Fred?'

'OK, Captain,' he replied.

'May I say a brief prayer with you, Fred?'

'Of course you can,' he replied.

Putting my arm around him I simply prayed, 'Dear Father, please give Fred the desire to have Jesus in his heart.'

'I do want to have Jesus in my heart,' Fred responded.

I then opened my eyes to see Geoff, now very emotional, give Fred several firm punches in the chest. 'Then just ask him, Fred, just ask him,' he pleaded.

'Please, Jesus, forgive me and come into my heart,' is all Fred said. It was as if the heavens broke open. The words had hardly left Fred's lips when Geoff started to weep and Fred broke down and I joined them. The Holy Spirit came down upon us in power and the Lord Jesus came and entered Fred's heart.

We spent some time in prayer and praise and tears, then the three of us went to the kitchen to tell the Alpha course helpers who, on finishing their discussion, had sent the rest of the group home, only to suddenly discover that the captain had only half done the job he had started. They were busy clearing up the mess I had left as we popped our heads round the door and told them the story. On hearing of Fred's decision they were elated and stopped what they were doing to embrace him. Seeing the state that Fred was in when they did that touched me deeply.

Meanwhile, Geoff was wondering what we ought to do with Fred that night. He took me to one side. 'I know it sounds bad, but I really don't feel that I should take him back to stay with me,' Geoff said.

'Actually, I've been thinking about that too. I know it sounds awful, but I just feel that on this occasion we are to leave him in God's care.' The weather was warm and dry as we locked the hall. It was too late for there to be any buses, so I drove the 13 miles to Geoff's home, while Fred went off to the park to sleep, exuberant in his new experience of Jesus.

The following day I met Fred at lunchtime. His shoes were broken and beyond repair, so I had brought him a pair of mine. I then took him into a café for a meal.

'Did you sleep OK?' I asked as we walked along.

'No, worse than normal in fact,' he replied.

'I'm so sorry,' I answered, thinking that he would have spoken of a superb night with an inexplicable peace!

'Don't be,' Fred said, 'it was great. Every time I woke up and looked at the stars, I thought of how blessed I am and spent the time praising the Lord and thanking him!'

I was stunned, amazed. Listening to Fred I was aware that God had planted something very real and wonderful in the heart of my friend. This was not the Fred I had known for four years.

Many in the church who heard what had happened to Fred began praying for his future. I met him again the following day and offered to get him lunch again. He told me the shoes were very comfy, adding, 'I was thinking as I walked along, this time last week I would never have dreamed I'd be walking in the captain's shoes!' We both laughed. I then told him how utterly convinced I was of his conversion and how, as he had truly placed himself in God's hands, God himself would make a way for him and open doors to a brand new life. I was praying, 'Hurry, Lord, please hurry.'

'I know he will, Captain, it's been such an incredible two days. This morning I woke up so thirsty, but when I met a fellow alcoholic in the park and he offered me a full can of drink I refused it. I know it was the Lord that saved me from taking it.'

We entered the same café that I had taken him the day before and there, eating his dinner, was a man named Steve, one of two men I had met while Christmas carolling outside a local supermarket. They were Christians from London, who were building a house in town. They stayed in a caravan they had on the building site during the week and returned to their homes in London each weekend. It was good to see Steve again, we had met several times since Christmas and I had discovered him to be a deep, Bible-loving man of God.

I went over to where Steve was sitting and said hello. 'That's amazing,' he said. 'I never, ever come in here at lunchtime, but as it's bank holiday weekend I decided to pack up work early and get some lunch before I travel back to London this afternoon to have some more time with my daughter, and lo, I bump into you.' I introduced him to Fred and told him that he had given his heart to Jesus two days earlier. 'Brilliant,' Steve said.

'Can Fred share your table?' I asked.

'Of course,' he answered. Fred sat down and I went and ordered and paid for Fred's lunch. I then told Fred that Steve was a builder and Steve that Fred was a master bricklayer. They looked at each other in amazement.

Then Steve asked him, 'Do you need somewhere to stay?'

'Wow, do I need somewhere to stay!' Fred replied, surprised at the question.

'Look, I'll wait while you eat your meal and then we'll pop to the supermarket and get some more food in and you can stay in my caravan. I will be away until Tuesday and my partner has moved out. I'll catch up with you when I get back.'

'But you don't even know me,' said Fred, astounded at what he had heard.

'You are my brother, mate,' was Steve's only reply.

That evening I collected Fred from the caravan to take him to our home for a bath, a meal and a change of clothing. Steve had still not left for home when I got there. They had talked and prayed all afternoon and discovered they had a lot in common. Fred later told me that even in the café, as Fred ate his dinner and they talked together, Steve had been so affected by Fred's testimony that he had to go out into the street for a couple of minutes to stop himself breaking down in tears.

Fred remained in the caravan with Steve for a year before being rehoused in a lovely flat by the very housing association that had evicted him. Why did they agree to that? Because of the sense of responsibility that his new faith had given him, Fred felt he ought to start paying back what he owed his previous landlord, a housing association, despite his benefit being a meagre one, and despite the fact that his old landlord would obviously never allow him a tenancy again (or so he thought).

Chapter 12

Three Alcoholics

'Is that The Salvation Army?'

'Yes.'

'Please can you help me? My son-in-law is an alcoholic and has been drinking solidly for ten days now. He's not looking after himself and won't even get out of bed. The doctors have given up on him and I just don't know what to do. You are my last resort. Please will you come and see him?'

I had an hour to spare and so I jumped into my car and drove the two miles to the village praying, 'Help, Lord. If the experts have given up on him what can I possibly do?'

'His name is Mick, he's upstairs in his room,' Lucy said, having greeted me at the door of a large and beautiful house, with its well kept garden and neat lawns.

'Does he know that I'm coming?' I asked. Her reply was negative so I asked her if she would go up and check that he wanted to see me. I may be six foot five inches tall, but I didn't know whether he was a foot taller and a martial arts expert at that. She returned and said that he was willing to speak to me.

I knocked and entered his room and said, 'Hello.'

Mick's immediate reaction to seeing me was to declare, 'I don't believe in God and religion.'

In response I merely asked if I could sit on the edge of his bed as there was not an empty chair there. He agreed that I could and so I sat down and introduced myself. Mick was in his late 40s, unshaven with thick glasses, a university-educated, professional man, a chemist for a large company, in fact.

We chatted and I discovered that he and his wife had sold their house, and that his mother-in-law had also sold hers so that they could buy and share a much bigger property. All went well for a time until tragically, two years ago, his wife (Lucy's daughter) was taken ill and died. Mick was so distraught that he hit the drink big time.

While we chatted and got to know each other I noticed a number of Beatles CDs alongside his bedside radio/CD player, so we talked about the pop music of our youth, Mick being not that much younger than I. Having expressed my concern for him and my willingness to visit should he want me to, I asked if he would let me pray with him.

'I know that you think that it's all a load of nonsense, but if you would just bear with me like you might a child who believes in Father Christmas, I would appreciate it,' I said.

'Please yourself!' he replied.

My prayer was merely an admission of my uselessness, an expression of my concern for Mick and a pleading to the Lord to do something. In the midst of my prayer Mick suddenly burst into tears, which made concentration on my part very difficult. He didn't just cry, he wailed. I finished praying and he was inconsolable. Through the tears he thanked me for coming. I didn't know what to say and so just shook his hand and left him weeping. When I reached the bottom of the stairs, Lucy was waiting for me.

She led me into the kitchen and asked, 'What on earth is happening up there?'

'He's crying,' I said.

'What do you mean? Mick never cries, even when he's drunk.'

'Well he's crying now,' I replied.

'I don't understand. What did you do?'

'I didn't do anything, all I did was pray,' I answered.

Lucy, in her 80s, then told me her story. Mick had not been to work for quite some length of time, but he was still being paid. The trouble was that he was drinking all the money away and not paying the mortgage. She was desperately worried. I tried to console her and encourage her, but felt that I had no real answer to give her, other than my listening ear and concern. I told her that I would not impose myself on them, but that if she wanted me to visit at any time I would come.

A week later, having heard nothing from her, I telephoned Lucy just to let her know that I hadn't forgotten her.

'It's a miracle, a miracle,' she said.

'What is?' I asked.

'He hasn't drunk a drop since you were here,' she replied. 'He remained in bed for a couple of days after you left and then he started to eat again. A few more days after that, he got himself out of bed and bathed and shaved himself. Now he gets up the moment he wakes up, gets washed, eats breakfast and gets outdoors and busies himself in the garden all day. It's marvellous. He's never stopped drinking without help before.'

I had cause to drive past their house the following Sunday afternoon and so I stopped and rang the doorbell. Lucy came to the door and hugged me.

'He still isn't drinking,' she said. 'Would you like to see him?'

'Of course!' I replied.

She led me round to the back garden where Mick was sitting in the sunshine, on a white plastic garden chair at a white plastic table. We chatted over a cup of tea. He looked such a different person. After an hour I apologised that I needed to leave to prepare myself for conducting evening worship. He asked the whereabouts of our hall and the time of the service.

'I might come.' he said.

'Pigs might fly,' I thought. Up until that time I had rarely known an alcoholic keep a promise, and all of us who are officers, I am sure, are regularly meeting people who say that they will come to one of our meetings yet never, ever do!

I left Mick in the garden, hoping but not expecting that he would come. However, just in case he did come, my wife and I got to the hall early. To my surprise and delight, Mick was the first to arrive. As he hovered outside the door, we went out and welcomed him in.

At the end of the meeting, when the appeal was made for anyone to respond and accept God's salvation in Jesus, he was the first to come forward. He knelt and wept as my wife counselled him. Many of the congregation went to him afterwards and

81

welcomed him and promised him support and he left with a great smile on his face.

During the week that followed, I made time to go to his village and pop my head round the door again and again he was in the garden. This time my reception was very different. In place of a warm greeting was a pointed, wagging finger.

'Before you say anything, let me make it clear, if you think that you've converted me, think again,' he said quite aggressively.

I was taken aback as I cobbled together a reply. 'Mick, I don't convert anyone. I don't know what is going on inside you. All I know is that on Sunday night you met with the living God and you responded positively to him. It seems to me that since then you have been back-pedalling. Do you want to talk to me about it?'

He made no further comment on the subject. He then relaxed and we chatted quite amicably together about all sorts of other things before I prayed with him and left. After that Mick only occasionally came to the services and never moved any further spiritually. In fact he retreated back to where he started, unwilling to surrender and truly allow God to reign. He also took to the bottle again.

I would visit Lucy, who was often at her wit's end. Eventually she managed to get him to sell their home, and with its proceeds she bought a bungalow and Mick bought a small terraced house. From time to time I visited Mick. I would pray and he would weep, but resolutely his pride prevented his surrender. I met his parents – lovely, retired people who obviously loved their son and who were much distressed over him. They would persuade him to go and get 'dried out', and he would be fine for a few weeks, then he would be back drinking again.

I spoke to the local Alcoholics Anonymous group in the town who told me that they could not help him unless he desired their help. Nothing saddened me more than to spot him in town, walking home from the off-licence with a transfixed stare on his face, carrying a plastic bag containing his death sentence.

His mother, who loved him greatly, phoned me one morning. He had told her not to come round to his house so regularly and that it was enough for her to just to pop in at weekends. In response, she respected and conformed to his wishes, but she told me how, visiting him the previous Sunday, she had discovered him lying dead on the front-room carpet, having choked on his own vomit some days earlier, undiscovered.

I often met Eddie round the town. He was quick to tell me that he was a Catholic and that he prayed and read his Bible and was a believer, but it soon became clear that he had a drinking problem. He was in his 40s and had been a chef in the British Army but was now unemployed. One day he asked me if I would come to his flat to talk. There I met his live-in girlfriend, Claire, and the hamsters, rats and budgerigars they kept as pets. The flat smelt bad. They asked many questions about Jesus and faith and I gave them a Bible and a *Jesus* video (a film of the life and ministry of Jesus based on the Gospel of Luke), and they allowed me to pray with them.

Following my visit, they started to come to meetings occasionally on a Sunday, and then they joined the corps Alpha course. On the third week Eddie arrived at the Alpha course drunk, to the discomfort of the other people there and the embarrassment of Claire. I had great difficulty persuading him to leave.

He later phoned me to say that he was sorry and also to tell me that he had a job. He lost the job after just a few weeks. He managed to get other jobs and with each one he would do well for a while, be reliable and consistent, with his culinary skills appreciated by his employers, before again taking to the bottle. Within a short while he would then be asked to leave. He stopped attending Sunday worship, but would telephone me or meet me in the street and ask me to visit him. I did so on many occasions. We would talk about his life, his future and his need of help and I would pray with him.

He would attempt to hide his carrier bag of bottles if I met him returning from the off-licence. At other times he would stop drinking for several weeks and turn up at the hall, saying he had decided to join. Then Claire left him to move in with another man, he lost his flat and became homeless. He was beaten up by a group of youths one night and was hospitalised.

I visited him in hospital. He looked terrible. I pleaded with him to visit me when he came out. He visited once, just for some food. I then heard that he had been found dead in a back alley, having had a heart attack at 43 years of age.

———————————

After years of misery and stress, Nigel's wife could no longer stand his continual antisocial behaviour and so she locked him out of the house. They were both in their 50s and had two grown-up children. She was a secondary school headmistress. He was a gifted teacher of English Literature and French, and a brilliant guitarist too.

He spent one night in a local hostel for the homeless and in the morning they ejected him for breaking the rules. He then booked into bed and breakfast accommodation. I was first made aware of him when a public house landlord rang me and told me of this stranger who had booked a room for bed and breakfast and was now sitting in the lounge distraught and in tears. To the landlord he seemed possibly suicidal. By the time that I got to the public house in a village not far from town, Nigel had left.

A day or two later a member of the public contacted one of our soldiers who went and found Nigel in a much distressed state. Nigel agreed to be taken to one of our Salvation Army hostels in London and to accept help there for his alcoholism. The soldier, together with his wife, drove Nigel up to London that same evening. Sadly, Nigel did not stay there more than a night or two and was soon back in town. Up until that time I had not met him and would not have recognised him if I had.

On Friday evenings I used to visit a number of the local public houses in town with *War Crys*. One night, at my last port of call, the Park Tavern, I got into conversation with a group of men sat round a table. They were very pleasant and one of them expressed his personal gratitude to the local Salvation Army and to two members in particular, a husband and wife, who had recently helped him. I was obviously curious and discovered that the man I was speaking to was Nigel, the man who I had heard so much about during the preceding week or so. He told me that he had managed to rent a small flat in town. I asked if I could visit him and he responded gladly to the suggestion, giving me his address.

He was charming and amiable and, as we got to know each other, we had many discussions about literature, the state of the world and Jesus. He would have spells without drinking and felt that he could conquer it himself, even though he was a very intelligent and articulate man who knew his track record of failure through decades.

He came to a meeting at the Army one Sunday night and was so moved that he decided there and then to make it a regular thing and to come every week. I visited him during that week and he asked if any of the youngsters he had seen there might wish to learn guitar. I told him about the worship group we were forming and he said that he would love to be involved and help us. He had been part of a rock group in his younger days.

Like many an alcoholic's desires, dreams and intensions, sincerely meant when spoken, Nigel's came to nothing. He only came to worship on two further occasions.

I would periodically meet Nigel in the public house on a Friday night, though, and he would reiterate his good intentions, and with his brimming refilled pint glass on the table before him claim that he did not have an alcohol problem with beer, only with spirits. I still continued to visit him in his flat, sometimes letting myself in by pulling the string to which the door key was tied through the letter box, because he was laid out on the floor, too drunk to crawl any closer to the door to let me in.

On many an occasion I would drag him on to his bed and make him a cup of tea and sit with him. He would sometimes cry. But like the other two cases described above, there seemed to be a pride barrier. Though they all admitted that they had a drink problem, their lives seemed to deny their verbal confession. There was a sense in which each of them remained in denial. Even those who did go to Alcoholic's Anonymous made only temporary progress before discontinuing their visits and then relapsing.

Nigel told me one evening that he was selling his flat and buying a cottage in the Welsh countryside. He was going back to his roots, the land of his birth. He thought it might help by providing him with a new start. I and others who cared for him felt otherwise. He was grateful to the people at the corps who had supported him and he said that he would stay in touch. It was another broken promise. Tragically, a year later, Nigel's wife telephoned me to say that he had been found dead in his cottage and that they were bringing his body back to our town. She asked if I would be willing to conduct the funeral, which I was. I met Nigel's wife and two daughters – a lovely family, weighed down with guilt, in much need of reassurance. Everybody I met at his funeral spoke highly of him and, like me, were greatly upset at the waste of such a gifted man.

Three deaths of three alcoholics in less than 18 months. There is a cost to love – pain to be born and a burden to be carried, as only those who love know.

Chapter 13

Almost Persuaded

Jimmy was a neighbour who lived a few doors from us. When we first moved into our home I went to the local library and photocopied the entries of those people who lived in our cul-de-sac from the electoral roll so that my wife and I could pray for them all by name. Knowing their names also made any invitations I might want to make to corps events more personal.

Several neighbours whom we got to know did come along from time to time. Among them were Jimmy and his wife Jane. We had had several interesting conversations about faith, God and Jesus during the couple of years we had been neighbours and, as a result of questions they asked me, I offered them a copy of the *Jesus* video to watch. They were a little reluctant but took it anyway. Having watched it, they expressed surprise at some of the things that they discovered about Jesus, what he said and what he did. Following this we shared further conversation and I answered more questions. My hopes were high.

In the midst of all of this, one morning after a very busy Easter weekend, we looked through the kitchen window to see an ambulance arrive at our friends' home. We discovered afterwards that Jimmy had been taken into hospital having suffered a stroke which had affected his sight and mobility.

I was really angry with God. I had felt that God the Holy Spirit had been speaking to Jimmy and Jane and opening them up to the truth about Jesus and that he was leading them to himself. I could see them warming in response to the Spirit and the distinct possibility of them accepting Jesus as their Saviour in the not too distant future. Now, with Jimmy struck down with a stroke, my hope was all but dashed and destroyed.

It was a strange week because three of our soldiers and adherent members had died within days of each other as we approached Easter and I found myself conducting funerals on three consecutive afternoons after Easter, with each of the committals at a crematorium 12 miles away.

Following the second one on the Thursday I said to my wife that I felt that we needed to go and visit Jimmy in hospital instead of travelling back home. The hospital was in a town ten miles from both our home and the crematorium we were standing in. We arrived at the hospital, found the ward and were directed by the ward sister to Jimmy's bed. He was snoozing, but the sister, despite our request to let him sleep on, woke him. He was pleased and surprised to see us, telling us of all that he had experienced since he had come in three days earlier.

'My sight's coming back although it's not clear and I don't have any side vision. I was able to watch the football match on my mini screen last night, Manchester United against Juventus. It was the UEFA Champions League semi-final away and they beat Juventus 3-2. It was brilliant!' he said.

'You were able to watch it all on that small screen?' I asked, as he held up his little portable television for me to see (televisions at each bed were yet to be provided at that hospital then).

'Well, sort of,' he laughed. 'I could see the players all running around, but with my limited vision I just couldn't see the ball!' We continued to talk and joke. It was so good to see him in such good spirits. 'I've been having the physio lady visit me to exercise my legs; they got me out of bed this morning just to see if I could stand. They said that they were very pleased and are going to take me down to the gymnasium to start me walking tomorrow.'

'Brilliant!' I said. 'That really is good news. You are doing extremely well so soon after your stroke. It is amazing.'

'That's what the doctor said,' he responded. After further conversation with Judy and myself about the prognosis and how his wife and son were coping with the shock of it all, we felt it was time to leave him and so I asked him if he would like me to pray with him. He was silent for a minute.

'It doesn't matter, I won't be offended if you would prefer that I didn't,' I responded.

'No, that will be all right, thank you.'

I then thanked the Lord for all that he had done for Jimmy since he had entered the hospital and acknowledged that we were confused as to why it had happened, why God had allowed it. I asked that he would comfort and be near to Jimmy's wife and son and that they would be aware of his love. Finally, I prayed that God would come with his healing power to Jimmy and make him well and aware of his peace and presence.

With one or two more sentences of concern for the other patients and staff I concluded my petition and opened my eyes. Jimmy was staring coldly at me. I offered to shake his hand and he didn't move. I thanked him for his company, a little confused at his countenance, wondering whether offering to pray or the words that I had uttered in my prayer had somehow offended him. The gap between the bed and the wall was particularly narrow, so I needed to get out of it for Judy, who had been standing at the bottom of the bed, to get up close to him to shake his hand.

As I faced Judy and shuffled towards her, she pointed to Jimmy and said, 'He's beckoning you, Howard. He wants you to go back to him.'

I looked round, again confused. We had been talking together for almost an hour and he had had only minimal difficulty with his speech, yet now he was silent, just beckoning me with a nod of his head and what seemed a severe expression on his face. I returned to where I had been standing and he continued to nod, so I leant closer to him, wondering what he was going to say. I felt that he didn't want anyone else to hear because he was going to give me a telling-off for some reason. But it turned out to be quite the contrary.

'When you spoke I felt heat on my head,' he whispered.

'Heat on your head?' I asked.

'Yes, it was really hot as if there was a radiator above me. It was a real burning sensation.' The look on my face must have made him feel that I did not believe him.

'I'm serious,' he added. 'I'm not stringing you along, I'm not joking. The heat on my head came all the way down me, through my head, my neck and down my arms. What do you think that was?' he asked. We looked at each other in silence. I knew he wasn't joking. Just looking at his face and listening to the intensity in his voice told me that.

I didn't know quite what to say and let out the first thing that entered my head, 'God does things like that sometimes.'

We each said our goodbyes, but he seemed mesmerised, in another world. As we left him and looked back through the window, he was still staring into space.

'He looks stunned,' I said to Judy. 'I don't know what God did, but he just did something amazing to Jimmy. He's zapped him. He's zapped him in the nicest of ways, but he's zapped him nevertheless.'

Jimmy was not in hospital very long. He made great progress and when he got home I went across the road to visit him. Jane invited me in and made me a coffee and we sat together in the lounge.

'He's in bed, he gets very tired and sleeps a lot,' she said.

'I'm not surprised,' I replied, 'he's been through a lot.' She offered to wake him, but I said that I would come another time when he was awake.

'What happened?' she then asked.

'What do you mean, what happened?'

'Jimmy said that you said something, a prayer or something, and something happened to him while you were talking.'

'I don't know exactly *what* happened, you will have to ask Jimmy about that,' I responded. 'All I do know is that I asked God to bless and heal Jimmy and make him aware of his presence and I guess what Jimmy experienced was God answering my prayer.'

'I've never heard anything like it. Jimmy won't stop talking about it. His boss came this morning to see how he is doing and Jimmy went on and on to him about what happened when you spoke that prayer.'

As I listened to her I was amazed. Only a week ago I had been angry with God for letting this happen to Jimmy. Yet what happened set the stage for one of the most incredible experiences of Jimmy's life. What happened could only be attributed to God, his power, his mercy. No one else could get the credit for it or be given the glory. It reminded me of the story of the death of Lazarus, where Jesus tells us that what happened to Lazarus was for God's glory so that God's Son might be glorified through it (John 11:4).

I really desired to see such things happen more frequently so, like many another foolish man, I tried to analyse exactly what it was that I did and said that Thursday afternoon to bring about such a powerful blessing upon Jimmy. I felt that if I could reproduce my tiny part in the proceedings it would ensure the same or a similar powerful response by God in future.

We silly human beings do look for formulas, recipes by which we might control events, when the truth is that the wind of the Spirit blows wherever it (he) pleases (John 3:8). Sometimes God's answers to our prayers are immediate, as in the case of Peter sinking in the sea – short succinct prayer, rapid rescuing response (Matthew 14:30, 31); sometimes one might wait a almost a lifetime – as with Zachariah and Elizabeth, John the Baptist's pensioner parents.

When I next visited, Jimmy was still enthusing over what had happened to him. He spoke more of that than his illness and recovery. Apparently he told everyone he met about it.

'When I'm well I am going to come to church,' he said. I believed him.

Jimmy never did make a full recovery despite the amazing rapid progress that he made initially. His side vision never properly returned and so he had to give up driving and give up work. He was given a white stick because of his sight impediment, yet, despite his difficulties, he and Jane managed to take up their favourite pastime of ballroom dancing again.

Sadly, however, Jimmy never did come again to worship, which I thought was strange because they did come occasionally before that experience and were showing such an interest. But then again there were those whom Jesus healed who never returned to follow him, those whom he blessed miraculously who never did as he desired them to afterwards.

But the truth is that God never gives up on any of us. When we have encountered or known Jesus we can never pretend we haven't. Even when we put years between us and that encounter we can never forget the fact that it took place. Some of us who strayed from the Lord, perhaps in our youth, returned to God because, wherever we went and whatever we did, we were aware that we once experienced something more wonderful than we ever imagined possible, something that none of the experiences accumulated through the years were ever able to match.

One positive postscript to this story, regarding our prayers for those who lived in our street, is that a young mother of two children, who lived opposite our house, attended our corps Alpha course and committed her life to Jesus. I hear that, subsequently, following our departure from that corps and moving away from the town, her husband has begun attending worship with her.

Chapter 14

Temporary Freedom

One of the most wonderful places to minister is prison. Christ himself was imprisoned, so he knows what it is like. He who created the heavens and earth was confined to human flesh and also imprisoned in a Roman gaol before his death. He is in and is at work in prisons today.

I knew by the noise that the prisoners were making as they filed into the chapel that it wasn't going to be an easy morning. Three men in the front pew made it clear from the beginning that they were there merely 'for a lark'. Throughout the first hymn, they sang (?) the wrong words loudly, out of tune and out of time. As the service continued I could quite easily have asked the prison officers to remove the offending men. However, I felt my response to their antics was being watched as much as my words were being listened to by most of the other inmates.

As I concluded the service I prayed for the men before me, 'Dear Father God, these men are so precious to you,' I paused and the words, 'I'm not!' broke the silence, to the laughter of a small group of the men. I opened my eyes to see the large, macho, shaven-headed ringleader grinning from ear to ear, encouraged by his much amused small band of supporters.

Walking across to the front row of pews where they were seated, I said to the big man in the middle, 'Oh yes you are. You are more precious to God than you can ever imagine.' A lump grew in my throat and I felt tears welling up in my eyes, as I thought, 'If you only knew,' remembering how Jesus had said the same as tears welled up in his eyes at the sight of Jerusalem (Luke 19:42), and also when he spoke longingly to the woman by the well in Samaria (John 4:10). How many times have we, who know the Lord, ached for the non-believer in our company with the same sense of longing, 'If only you knew?'

I then explained how God had been showing him love all his life and how God's heart was so broken and his longing for him so great that he gave his own Son to die for him. I then completed my prayer. The atmosphere was now one of quiet and there was no more showing off, no more comments. The men left the chapel subdued and, as I shook hands with each prisoner, several thanked me for dealing with the disrespect. Though the service was little more than 30 minutes in length, I felt completely exhausted as the next group of men filed in for the second service.

There is no more exciting, stimulating or responsive congregation than those I find in prison. Thankfully, though, I have never again experienced such a hard time as that small, vociferous group gave me when the first service began that morning.

With the second – uneventful – service over, I went to the chaplain's office, collected my coat and went and waited by the gate for someone to let me out. I was somewhat eager to get home, relax and lubricate my parched throat. However, a young man came and asked to have a word with me.

He commented on what he had heard in the chapel and then said, 'The opposite to found is lost, isn't it?'

'That's right,' I replied.

'When you speak of someone being lost, do you mean they are going to Hell?'

I hesitated, wondering what was coming next. 'Er, yes,' I again replied.

'Do you believe in Hell?' he then asked.

'Yes,' I answered.

'Did Jesus believe in Hell?'

'Yes, he spoke about it more than anyone else in the Bible, but people often fail to realise that because he also spoke of the love of God and Heaven more than anyone else in the Bible.'

'I don't believe in Hell,' he then said, emphatically.

'Well, you can believe whatever you want to believe,' I said.

94

'But I've always thought that that's where I'm going.'

That sounds contradictory, but there are those who hold strong convictions that they would defend adamantly who also sense 'something' within them whispering that the view they hold just isn't true and they are not at rest, despite their ability to win an argument with an opponent.

The lad continued, 'I'm not all bad you know. I know what I have done is wrong, but I'm not all wicked. I do far more good things than I do bad things. Surely God knows that?'

I replied, 'He does know that and he is pleased with the good that he sees, but there remains one problem, a problem for both you and me.'

'What's that?'

'Whatever the good you do, and Jesus was aware that even the worst of people were capable of doing good [Luke 11:13], your sin disqualifies you from Heaven and qualifies you for Hell.'

His response was an echo of the voice of a jailer in a prison nearly 2,000 years ago, asking, 'What must I do to be saved?' [Acts 16:30].

I told him what he needed to do and how he could be saved there and then on the prison landing if he did it.

'I'll think about it,' he said.

'Think about it by all means, but don't leave it until it's too late,' I told him. 'Satan is clever at agreeing with our best intentions, but then encourages us to add the word "tomorrow" to them.'

He returned to his cell with a Gospel and an agreement that I visit him when I next came to the prison, which was on the following Friday afternoon.

When I entered the cell I knew something had happened. His face shone. I discovered that, following our encounter on the landing the previous Sunday, he had read the Gospel and on the Wednesday had knelt by his bed (fortunately he was in a cell on his own), asked God to forgive him his sin and invited Jesus to be his Saviour. He had then requested a Bible from prison's full-time chaplain and had already read half the New Testament!

We sat on his bed and together we went through a list of questions he had prepared for me from what he had read. He asked what the Sabbath was, who Elijah was, what the Passover was. He told me of how he was sleeping properly for the first time for years.

'No one ever told me any of this,' he said. 'I didn't know any of it,' he repeated, so excited at the treasure he had found. I was overjoyed at his joy but also saddened when he pointed to a photograph on his cell wall of a young man. 'He was my best mate, he was killed last year. He didn't know any of this stuff. What about him?'

I thought of the many people who claim to have known and loved the Saviour for a long time and yet seem to show so little interest or concern in the spiritual welfare and ultimate destiny of those about them. Here was a man who had only came to know Jesus a few days ago already expressing such concern for his 'mate'.

So it was that each week I visited Wayne in his cell to see how he was progressing in his walk with Jesus. He couldn't wait to share with me what he had discovered, as though I knew nothing of what he had found. And he was hungry to know more. He always had a host of questions for me.

It was only as I got to know him more that I discovered an even greater significance as to what God had done in the heart of this young man.

I noticed how respectful and fearful of him the other prisoners who shared the landing of his wing were, and the deference they showed him. On one occasion during recreation, when the men were let out of their cells, I was walking along the landing towards Wayne's open cell door when three men on the walkway opposite started calling out defamatory remarks and abusive names to me.

Although I did not like what they were saying, I turned and accepted their insults with a smile. As I turned back to look towards where I was going, Wayne shot out of his cell in front of me and, with fiery anger in his eyes, leant across the handrail, pointing aggressively towards them, shouting, 'Who was it? Who was it? Tell me who it was, Mr Webber.' I looked back towards where he was pointing and saw the three men now frozen with fear, the grins having evaporated from their faces.

'Wayne, Wayne, let it be,' I pleaded, as I led him back into his cell and sat myself on his bed. 'That's not the way we deal with things now.'

'You're not to take it! They're not going to talk to you like that! They need to understand that you're my friend and no one talks to my friend like that!' he responded.

'Wayne, it's not important. If someone is rude and abusive for no reason, it is they that have the problem. You must pray and ask God to bless those who curse you, like Jesus told us to, like Jesus did on the cross.'

Wayne was short but stocky, with a very solid frame – the result of his bodybuilding programme. Some years earlier he had won the title Mr Nottingham. He was a drug dealer, in fact the biggest drug dealer and gangster in the city where he lived, but he was now determined to turn over a new leaf when he left prison. He had a girlfriend, Nisha, who was the mother of his youngest child – a daughter named Sunnie, nine months old – and he also had two older children from previous relationships. Nisha was a young, teenaged, mixed-race woman and a photo of her and her baby daughter was on his cell wall. He was very proud of her and the fact that she was a model.

Over the next few months, I popped in to see him most Friday afternoons for an hour to monitor his progress and chat through some of the issues in his complicated life. Then one Friday evening I had a telephone call rather late at night from the full-time chaplain. He sounded very troubled as he started to explain his reason for calling me so late. Apparently the police had come to Lincoln Prison from Nottingham, Wayne's home town, to see him and to have the chaplain break the news to Wayne that his girlfriend had drowned their little baby and hanged herself in their flat. I was stunned as the chaplain continued and told me that Wayne had been taken to the prison hospital for observation just in case receiving such terrible news might cause him to be suicidal.

'Seeing that you have a lot to do with him and he knows you well, I just wondered whether you might come in tomorrow and spend some time with him?' he added. I obviously agreed to the request and put the telephone down, stunned by the news.

I switched the television on as the regional news broadcast was imminent and Nottingham and Lincoln (where I lived) were in the same region. Sure enough, the report confirmed that the bodies of a woman and her baby had been found, and that the police were not looking for anyone else. They showed the block of flats where she lived, cordoned off with lots of blue police tape. I slept very little that night.

When I got to the prison the following morning I made my way to the hospital and the officer I met unlocked a room for me to meet with Wayne. I had no idea what to say when they brought him in. We just embraced and I just said that I was so sorry.

We spent the next hour in silence, him on one side of the room, I on the other. I could not think of one thing to say that didn't sound banal. I was also very angry with God and somewhat confused that Wayne should be so tested so early on in his Christian life.

The officer then came in and told us we had five more minutes. I asked Wayne if I could pray for him. He agreed. As I said 'Amen' the door opened and the officer beckoned him towards it. As he walked through the door he turned and thanked me for coming.

We both welled up with tears when he then added, 'I know this sounds strange, but I still feel that God loves me.'

I found out where and when the funeral would be and drove to Nottingham. It took me a while to find the church. The sun was shining brightly as I stepped into what seemed to be a huge cavern of a place, very dark. There were three or four people scattered among the pews. I sat at the end of a row by the aisle so that Wayne might catch a glimpse of me and know I was there for him, just in case we didn't get to see each other afterwards. I was sad at the fact that there were so few people there.

Time passed slowly. It was a depressing silence. Then suddenly the large doors opened with quite a bang, and I looked round to see the sun's rays bursting through the doorway like hot rods of gold reaching down to the floor from some elevated furnace. A white coffin was carried in containing mother and child. The vicar walked ahead of the coffin reciting a passage of Scripture, and Wayne followed behind it, handcuffed to one of the two prison officers who accompanied him.

There then followed a huge crowd of people that flowed like a river in flood down the central aisle, spilling out into the pews to the left and the right. As I looked into the faces of the mass of people now gathered round me, I wondered if the whole of the city's underworld had come.

When the service ended and I followed the crowd out into the sunshine I found Wayne waiting to talk to me and introduce me as his friend to his mum and dad. Despite his attempts to hide it, he could not conceal his unbearable pain.

The following Friday, back in his cell, Wayne thanked me for making the effort to attend. I asked him lots of questions about the different characters I had observed. He told me he was still praying and reading his Bible and wondered how he would have coped without his new faith. I told him I only wished that his friends could know the Saviour that he had discovered. He agreed.

I also said how I wished that I was free to join him when he left prison and returned home, so that I could get to know his friends when he got out. He explained that that would be difficult as they all treated him with respect because they feared him, whereas I did not have any fear of him. My presence and the fact that I teased him would undermine his position.

Wayne had a split sentence, whereby he was allowed to go home for a month or so before either paying a hefty fine or serving a further term in an open prison. While he was out of prison, I had to go to a officers' meeting in Nottingham at William Booth Memorial Halls. Just before the meeting began I realised that I had left a folder I needed in my car, so I left the hall and stepped on to the zebra crossing outside to go and get it.

Then, suddenly, the driver of the car which had stopped for me to cross the road started sounding his motor horn in such an aggressive manner that it quite startled me. I was also confused because he *had* stopped to let me cross the road. However, when I looked at the windscreen of the vehicle I was amazed to see, despite the sun's reflective glare, that it was Wayne in the driver's seat! I ran to the driver's door as he opened his window.

'I can't believe it,' I said. 'What are the chances of you being around here and pulling up at the very zebra crossing that I am about to step on to in a city like this?' As I looked into his face I realised he was very agitated. 'What on earth's the matter, Wayne?' I asked.

'Everything's gone wrong since I got out, Mr Webber. Have you got time to talk?'

'Of course,' I replied.

'Jump in then,' he said.

I ran round to the passenger door, opened it and jumped in as he pressed hard on the accelerator and we sped away. Both he and I were amazed that we had bumped into each other as we had, just when he needed someone to talk to.

As we travelled along, I had no idea where he was taking me. Eventually he pulled up in a quiet road where nearly all the houses had been demolished and those left were boarded up. He told me of his many problems and the trouble he had had since leaving prison.

Knowing his girlfriend had died, one of his former girlfriends had been round to his flat in an effort to resurrect her relationship with him. He had refused to respond and, as a result, when he left his flat she had started smashing his windows. The noise had alarmed the neighbours so they then called the police. The very last thing he needed while he was out was the police on his case. And this was just one of the problems that he was trying to deal with. I had no simple answers.

'Mr Webber, you have no idea how hard it is out here,' he said. 'You'll never understand my world.'

My heart ached for him. Our worlds were poles apart. We can glibly tell someone to abandon the world they live in and step into a new world, but it is not an easy thing to do when all your friends, nearly all your neighbours and most of your family are in that world. It's the only world you've ever known and you cannot imagine another world or the new life that might await you there. After an hour, we prayed together. He said he felt a lot different and better for us meeting and took me back to the hall where he had picked me up.

'I bet you were worried when I drove you off and you didn't know where I was taking you?' he laughed.

'Actually I didn't worry, Wayne. You're my friend and I trust you,' I replied.

Wayne didn't pay the fine so went back into an open prison some miles from where I lived. Things were not the same. Spiritually, Wayne was struggling. I was still able to visit him every few weeks, but I had to do it by appointment and one day I telephoned the prison to arrange my visit only to discover that he had been released. I was sad that he never sent me a message to say he was leaving and he didn't leave a contact address.

I often thought of him and wondered where life had taken him. In the world that he lived in he had money and prestige, power and position, huge income, luxury car, property. As deplorable and immoral as his life may have been, what was the alternative to someone without qualifications, whose only friends were in the underworld and who was fast approaching middle age? Stacking shelves in a supermarket, labouring, cleaning, for a pittance?

Wayne reminded me of the soil where the thorns are in the Parable of the Sower. 'Still others,' says Jesus, 'like seed sown among thorns, hear the word; but the worries of this life, the deceitfulness of wealth and the desires for other things come in and choke the word' (Mark 4:18, 19). One thing certain about the seed that fell among thorns is that *it was* sown. When it comes to Wayne, the seed *was* sown. For a time, he really did know and love Jesus.

The rich young ruler found it too hard to walk away from all that he had to follow Jesus (Matthew 19:16-24). He never discovered the life, the abundant life, that he would have had if he had kept his focus on following Jesus. Often the unattractive way, the way we would not naturally choose – be it stacking shelves, labouring or cleaning – if it is what Christ would have us do, turns out to be the best way of all.

When we look at Christ's life and ministry and his desire to draw all people to himself – to save the world – we see that he had many disappointments. We have already mentioned the rich young ruler, but imagine preaching your heart out to express, at its deepest level,

101

the relationship that you wish to have with people, only to see them turn away from you in droves, to the point where you wonder whether those closest to you will stay with you (John 6:66).

Then there are the nine lepers that did not return to thank Jesus after he had given them what they desired and needed (Luke 17:11-19) and also those he healed who blatantly refused to obey his command to keep quiet about it (Mark 7:36).

No servant is greater than his master, so why should we be surprised at the disappointments that we experience? There may be more failures than successes. There may be far, far more who never respond than who show an interest (that has certainly been my experience). But with all the disappointments and heartache and sorrow they bring, the joy that comes even once in a while when someone responds to Christ and stays and grows in grace and bears fruit makes it all worthwhile.

> Come, tell me all that ye have said and done,
> Your victories and your failures, hopes and fears;
> I know how hardly souls are wooed and won;
> My choicest laurels are bedewed with tears.

Edward Henry Bickersteth

Chapter 15

Disappointment To Delight

I walked up the garden path and knocked on the door of the white wood and glass porch extension and waited, wondering who would come to the door. After a few minutes' delay the inner door opened and a thin, short man with tanned complexion, in his late 50s, came through into the sunlit porch to open the outer door.

'Ron?' I questioned.

Yes, I am. Can I help you?' he asked.

'You might be able to,' I replied. 'I'm the local Salvation Army officer,' I added, giving him my name.

'I know. I see you around and hear a lot about you,' he replied.

'Oh!' I thought. 'I wonder what he's heard?' Then I said, 'Well, we have a minibus, but the old man who has driven it for us for quite some time has been very ill and, although he is better than he was, he doesn't feel that he will be able to do it anymore.'

At this point a big grin spread across Ron's face that I found somewhat offputting. I guessed immediately that he had worked out the reason I was there.

'Go on,' he said, still smiling as I hesitated.

'And I have been told,' I continued, 'that you drive a minibus for Age Concern and that you just might be willing to drive our minibus for us.'

'Come in,' he then said, beckoning me into the porch and closing the door behind me. On a small table that was standing in the corner, next to a vase of flowers, lay a *Watchtower* magazine. As he turned to lead me into the lounge he caught me looking at it and added, 'I'm not one of those! I'm not a JW!' [Jehovah's Witness]. I made no comment as he led me into the room and offered me an armchair.

'Take a seat. Would you like a cup of tea?' he asked.

'Yes, please,' I answered.

He strolled into the kitchen, calling back, 'I'm semi-retired, well sort of. I'll have to think about it. What days would you want me?'

I got up and joined him in the kitchen and told him.

'Can I come back to you on that?' he answered.

'Of course. If you can't do all I need, I'll be more than grateful for anything you can offer.'

We took our teas back into the lounge and sat and chatted.

'You've had the Jehovah's Witnesses around today then, have you?' I asked.

'No, no. I have a very good friend who is one, and he comes and chats and leaves me the magazine. He's been trying desperately to get me along to one of their meetings. I think he wants to convert me,' he chuckled. 'I do read the stuff. Some of it's quite good, quite interesting, but there's something that just doesn't seem right – something that I find disturbing.'

'In what way?' I asked.

'I don't really know,' came his reply.

'So what is it that you *do* believe?' I queried.

He laughed. 'I don't know really. I do believe there is a God. I can't believe that all this made itself. I'm sure that there is more to life than just being born, living and dying.'

After about an hour of conversation, as I prepared to leave, I suggested, 'Look, Ron, if ever you would like me to come round for us to chat some more, I'm happy to do so. I'm not a Bible-basher. I'm not going to try and get you into our church, but if it would help to talk through stuff, I'm more than happy to come and see you again.'

'You're a very busy man,' he responded. 'You've got far more important things to do than to sit here listening to me, people with more pressing needs who need your time.'

I assured him that that wasn't the case, and he promised to let me know his decision regarding driving the minibus for us. Sure enough, five days later, the phone rang and it was Ron to tell me that he would be willing to cover all the times I had told him of, but only until I found someone else to do it permanently. He also said that he had enjoyed our chat and that I was to pop in whenever I was passing. If he was in he would put the kettle on.

So it was that he became our minibus driver and I would call by every few weeks and share time with him. I met his lovely wife, much younger than him, and his two- year-old daughter. As I got to know him, he shared with me much about his life, including a great shadow of guilt that hung over him – something I would never have perceived from his bright and humorous demeanour. What also became clear was that he was a genuine seeker.

Still in need of a permanent voluntary driver, I advertised for one in our shop window. We had started a new work, a corps plant, in this small market town, and were using different venues for our various meetings. Not having a building of our own, there was little evidence that The Salvation Army was in town. As a result of prayer and the growing sense of needing to be physically available and a visible presence in the town we acquired a shop.

Our small congregation all agreed that the purpose of the shop was to be a means of interacting with people, not a money-making enterprise, although it would obviously need to pay its way.

The shop and the accompanying coffee shop became a hive of activity as well as somewhere that we could meet at the start of each day for prayer. People would come for counselling or company, and it also became a 'shop window' into the Kingdom. Incidentally, God had additional plans – it did make a lot of money. Within two years there was sufficient accumulated proceeds to purchase a piece of land in preparation for the day when a purpose-built centre was needed!

One day a 34-year-old man came in to the shop in response to the advert in the window and offered to drive our minibus. He said that he had been in the town a while and had felt drawn to us for months, but had resisted until he saw the note in the window. Having checked him out, I told him that I would introduce him to Ron, who would show him the ropes, minibus-wise.

We were about to commence worship the following Sunday when Andy came in to the school hall we were using! He seemed overwhelmed at the warmth of the welcome he received. During the following week, I introduced him to Ron, who took him out on his rounds picking up people from the outlying villages who relied on the minibus to come to worship and/or to various other activities we had.

The following Sunday, Andy was at worship again and, as it drew to a conclusion, he responded to the appeal to accept Jesus as his Lord and Saviour. We were all thrilled. A few days later I paid one of my occasional visits to Ron, who as yet had never joined us at worship, to see how he had got on with Andy and what he had made of him. I discovered that he and Andy had got on like a house on fire as they drove round the Lincolnshire countryside. I also heard that Andy's first visit to Sunday worship had made a deep impression on him and that they had had much spiritual conversation. Ron also told me how Andy had challenged him as to his standing before God. Ron said that he was quite forceful.

I responded with a smile by saying, 'That's amazing. What a cheeky chappy, to say that to you when he himself hadn't sorted out his own standing before God.' We both laughed.

'Andy certainly is a character,' Ron said, then added, 'I like the guy. The folks on the minibus love him, he comes over as very caring. Did you know that he has had drink and drugs problems?'

'Yes, he did share that with me,' I said. 'Oh, and by the way, Andy has made a commitment to God now. He made a decision on Sunday. I think that he challenged himself when he challenged you in the minibus last week!' Again we both laughed. Ron then allowed me to pray with him for the first time, telling me as I left that he would be with us on Sunday. Sure enough, when Sunday came, he was there.

Some weeks later Andy was taken ill with flu. He had no one to care for him, no family around. What family he did have were not only 20 miles away, but they did not want anything to do with him because of his previous life of drink, drugs and prison. He was ashamed of his past, but he didn't hide it from us. I visited him in his dingy, cramped, damp bedsit, at the top of a building that overlooked the market square. He looked terrible. He could hardly keep awake, so I checked that there was nothing he needed and, after a prayer left him, promising to call back later in the week when he was feeling better.

When I tried his door later that week I found it locked and could get no response when I knocked. I tried again, several times, and a few days later discovered that, despite all the love and support shown towards him by his new friends in the fellowship, some old friends sought him out while he was none too well and vulnerable and he accepted the drugs they offered him.

He didn't come near the shop or our worship for weeks. We had to make other arrangements for the minibus. Occasionally, members of the fellowship would bump into him in the town and express their great affection for him, even though he had let them down.

During this period, he also met up with an old drug-user friend, Scott, who tried to purchase some drugs from him. Andy had nothing for him and shared his desire to give up his old life! The result was that Andy returned to worship with this old friend the following Sunday, coming forward and kneeling at our penitent form[1] at the end of the meeting and weeping over what he had done.

Over the next few weeks Scott and then Ron also came forward to publicly commit their lives to the Lord Jesus Christ. The four of us then met regularly to look together at what being a true disciple of Jesus was all about. There was much evidence of real change taking place in their lives – a steadiness and reliability on the part of all of them. I even took them with me when I went preaching elsewhere. They would help by reading the Bible for me or giving their testimony in the meeting.

---

[1] At the front of a Salvation Army worship hall is a long purpose-built bench, a piece of furniture peculiar to The Salvation Army, which is referred to variously as a penitent form, a mercy seat or even a mourner's bench. One of its names is a reference to the golden mercy seat, the lid of the ark of the covenant, described in Exodus 25:22 (*King James Version*), where God says, 'I will commune with thee from above the mercy seat.' Thus, an appeal by a preacher to seek God or respond to God is often accompanied with an invitation to make a public acknowledgement of that response by the physical act of kneeling before God there. This humble posture can often be an aid to having a right spirit, a humble, contrite heart before God. It is only a piece of furniture. A Salvationist does not believe it to have special properties. In fact any chair could be used for the purpose.

One of the joys I had regarding Ron was that God had lifted the great, overbearing shadow of guilt that for so long had hung over him. 'I will always regret what I did, but I now know that I am forgiven and that what I did was forgiven by Jesus when he died on the cross,' he would say. 'It is no longer the heavy burden that it was.' But I remained somewhat concerned for the two younger men. I was also deeply concerned about the hovels they both lived in.

One day, while walking in the town, I was stopped in the street by a man I had never met before, who offered me a house in the town – a house that he owned and wished to rent out. I went to see it. It was a spacious and bright semi-detached cottage. The rent was less than our two guys were paying for their bedsits, so I found them and took them to see it.

'All we would need would be some cutlery and some furniture,' Andy said excitedly. Indeed, both Scott and Andy were more than grateful for this sudden, unexpected change in their fortunes. I left them to sort things out with the landlord and wandered back to the shop, where the manager surprised me by showing me a lovely cutlery set that had just been donated.

'Oh, and this gentleman's father,' she said, as she handed me a piece of paper with a name and telephone number written on it, 'has just died and he wants his father's house cleared. He would like it to be of some use to The Salvation Army and wondered whether you would ring him on this number as soon as possible if you are interested in it, otherwise he will offer it to someone else.'

I immediately rang the man, made an appointment and, with the box of cutlery under my arm, went off in search of Andy and Scott. When I found them they could not believe my news, the timing of the events of the morning, or the fact that the house to be cleared was in the very road where their new home was situated!

'If this isn't God speaking, I don't know what is!' one of them said.

They settled in and were very happy there. Things went well for some time. The two of them got on very well together. Both in the shop and with the minibus, or regarding anything else we asked him to do, Andy in particular proved himself to be a great asset, a willing and hard worker, entering into all that he did with great enthusiasm.

Also he was not backward in speaking out for Jesus and witnessing to the change in his life since accepting Christ, something he was prepared to do whomever he was with.

But he wasn't as strong as he wanted to be or tried to make out. With him, the spirit was indeed very willing, but the flesh was weak. Some months down the line, in a moment of weakness, he was offered some 'speed' by an old friend, an offer he foolishly accepted. He again withdrew himself from us and we were again unable to make contact with him, or Scott for that matter.

Again, it was several weeks before I eventually made contact with first Andy (he was in a mess) and then Scott. I discovered that they had fallen out with one another because Scott had become intolerant of Andy letting the drugs get the better of him. Nevertheless, parting from the mate who had introduced him to us had left Scott feeling very low, and he too was now struggling. For him, it was with his alcoholism.

I reminded them both how much their new friends cared for them, how God would never give up on them and that they both needed professional help, but I never saw either of them again.

Their unhappy landlord then sought me out, to find out if I knew where they had gone as they had 'done a moonlight flit' and left several weeks' rent outstanding. It was the first I knew of the fact that they had both left town and I was deeply disappointed that they had left without so much as a goodbye. I did my best to placate their angry landlord, but could not account for or excuse what they had done.

Two weeks later Ron, who continued to grow in his relationship with the Lord, was enrolled as an adherent member of The Salvation Army. The fellowship rejoiced at the evidence of Ron's growing relationship with God but was deeply saddened by Andy and Scott vanishing as they had.

*   *   *

I received an email out of the blue, forwarded to me from our Territorial Headquarters. It was from a chaplain of a prison in Derbyshire who was trying to trace me. Eleven years had now passed since my wife and I and those of our children still at home left Lincolnshire. We had then spent ten years in Kent, the rest of our children had left home and my wife and I were now living in East London.

In the email, the chaplain told me that a prisoner named Andy, someone who at one time had known me, wanted to make contact with me again. I spent some time wracking my brain to think of an Andy I had known in one of the various prisons I had ministered in. I could not think of one and I sent an email back to the chaplain telling him as much. An immediate reply told me that this Andy did not know me from prison, but from a time I had spent in Lincolnshire, many years previously.

Straight away I found the mental filing cabinet where the memories of Andy were filed away and let the chaplain know. He then told me why Andy was in prison, that he had come to Christ and was doing a sterling spiritual work among his fellow prisoners. He asked if I could give him an address to give to Andy so that he could write to me. Andy had been round to our previous home many times and shared meals with the family and, despite the seriousness of his crime for which he was now inside, I had no hesitation in allowing him to have our home address.

The following week Andy's first letter arrived. It included his memories of our time together, of him giving his life to the Lord, giving his testimony, 'Though my honesty may have made it a bit too graphic for some!' he wrote.

Quoting from his letter: *I lost my way, I fell back into my old sinful nature – Satan got hold of me. I let you down, I let a lot of people down who had come to know me. In the end I ran away to Lincoln to a bedsit. I left owing rent. I fell into despair, and fell into the traps the evil one had set for me. After a stay in Lincoln I moved back to Grimsby. Although I had not had a drink for years* [drugs were his problem when we knew him], *I wasn't sober in my mind. I started to drink again. I quickly spiralled into my previous alcoholic drinking, and although I tried to get sober, the evil one had me down and under his power.*

To cut a sad story short, during a drunken argument I attacked the love of my life and dearest friend. I didn't realise that I had hurt her. When I left her to go out I thought that she was OK. She wasn't. She died sometime later of abdominal bleeding. She too was an alcoholic and was considerably drunk at the time. I often think that maybe she didn't realise how badly hurt she was. I was arrested the following day for murder, and at a trial was sentenced to life imprisonment. The judge said that I was to serve a minimum of 9 years and 100 days. The judge accepted that I did not mean to kill her. He also accepted my remorse, the fact that I was very drunk at the time and that it was not a premeditated attack.

Looking back now at what happened, it was as if a dark force was behind what I did, possessing me to do such a thing. I remember thinking (when I had sobered up) that God had abandoned me and that I was destined to eternal damnation. I remembered you and my time with the Lord back then, and it was like despair at realising that I had been on the narrow path with you then, and now I felt I had blown my chance… So I lost all hope, and I wondered whether despair could get any worse. Oh it can and it did!

I arrived in this prison and for the first two years my life was one of hopeless despair. My heart cried out to the Lord, I was wracked with guilt, remorse and quite frankly incredulity that I was serving a life sentence for murder. Never in my wildest dreams did I think that I could be capable of doing what I did. I still saw it as an accident, I really did. Eventually, I found myself in the 'chokey' or punishment bloc, firstly because I tried to take my own life and, secondly, because I was in debt on the wing and my safety was at risk. Down there I just wanted to die, I was without hope, looking for the best way to secure a ligature so I could hang myself.

Then suddenly my heart spoke to me, sorry, as you know it was Jesus. He said to me, 'Ring your bell and ask the guard for a Bible.'

In my mind I said, 'Why, what is the point?'

My heart replied, 'Just do it!' So I did. The officer bought me a New Testament With Psalms *some time later, and as I read the Beatitudes I started to cry. It was self-pity, but I carried on. I couldn't stop reading. I went through Matthew, Mark and then, during Luke, came across the Parable of the Lost Son* [Luke 15:11-31]. *Something happened. The Lord showed me that he hadn't abandoned me. Suddenly I had hope in my heart, I was no longer afraid, something was massively different. I couldn't sleep, all I could do was read the Word, pray, read, pray.*

He then went on to tell me how he had then gone to chapel and recommitted his life to Jesus at the altar there. That was 12 months ago. Bringing me up to date, he told me how he is part of the chapel band, on a Christian nurture course and heavily involved in the Christian life of the prison.

I wrote back sharing my delight in the change that had taken place. He then began to phone me as well as exchange letters. He had no visitors and no contact with his family. I promised him I would visit if ever I was in the vicinity, and I kept in contact with the chaplain.

Some months later I discovered that a corps Easter retreat that I was conducting was going to be only ten miles from the prison that Andy was in. I contacted the chaplain to organise a visit and, as I was free on the Good Friday afternoon, he suggested I come then and asked me if I would like to preach in the chapel before meeting Andy.

What a privilege that was! The place was alive. What a delight to be reunited with my old friend, such a different person to the one I had known all those years previously, now single-minded in his passion for God. What a joy after the service to be introduced to four other inmates whom Andy had introduced to the Lord and to listen to them share their wonderful testimonies of what God had done and was doing.

Andy still has many years to serve, but he now looks on it to be a privilege to be where he is. He takes the opportunity to reach, in an incarnate way, other lost inmates who listen to him and his message of hope because he, too, is a prisoner.

When Andy walked out of our lives all those years ago, we couldn't see beyond what our human eyes could see. We did not know the nature of the seed that had been planted in Andy's heart while he was with our small fellowship – a seed that would remain buried for the next ten years before being reawakened into life by God's Spirit to bear fruit in abundance.

Chapter 16

In Christ's Classroom
(John 4:1-42)

I have learnt and still am learning many delightful lessons by just sitting in Christ's classroom, watching, listening. Please come and join me for one. The room isn't in a grey-walled edifice, a university college. It is not a red-bricked school classroom. There are no books or ballpoint pens, projectors or multimedia. We are in the open air watching Jesus.

It is one thing to read Scripture in the comfort of our armchairs but quite another actually to enter the situation of which we read. Particularly with the Gospels, we need to allow the Holy Spirit to lead us into the incident we are reading about, so that it becomes our personal experience. Only then can we begin to pick up Jesus' mood, his train of thought, his spirit and each nuance in his words and actions.

It is one thing to view things from a distance, even with the benefit of the powerful binoculars which modern Bible scholarship gives us, and quite another to be present at the scene, watching and listening, even participating as the sequence of events unfolds before us.

Sit beneath this tree here on this hot, dry, dusty day and watch what happens. It is noon and the sun is at its highest. There is not a soul about and there is a well just over there to the left, deserted of course at this time of day. In the distance I can see a group of people coming this way. As they come closer, I can make out more details.

I see the group move off along the Sychar road while one solitary person comes this way. It is a man who is obviously very tired. He makes his weary way to the well and slumps down beside the little surrounding wall. It is Jesus. He is weary, he is thirsty, he is hungry, and though he possesses the power of God to feed 5,000 people from near nothing he does nothing with that power for his own relief. Instead he sends his disciples to the town to purchase food, or is that the real reason?

As he sits there we see a woman come up to the well with a pitcher to draw water, and he is watching her too as she approaches. It's a strange time of the day to come to draw water. The common practice is for all the town's women to come late in the day when it is cool and when they can catch up on all the news and local gossip. Is she totally disorganised, in need of extra water, or is it that she has been rejected by the other women, a social misfit? No one labours in this heat by choice.

'Will you give me a drink?' asks Jesus. To her, just surprising words. To you and me, a cascade of colour and beauty – a bottomless well of delight.

'My, how God loves us!' I cry, when I see him sitting in the dust out of love for me – almighty God, all-knowing, everywhere-present, existing from eternity to eternity, who has only to breathe a whisper and the universe would be no more, sitting in the dust asking one of us for sustenance! The One through whom everything was created and for whom everything was created, rich beyond our mortal minds' comprehension, becomes poverty out of love!

His cot is lent him, his tomb is not his own, the ass for a triumphant entry into Jerusalem is but borrowed with the promise of a safe return. And yet it is he and he alone who can bring the relief that our thirsting, parched souls crave.

He presumes on her kindness, as one anticipating a positive response. He anticipates kindness. The virtue of kindness is assumed in a woman he already knows to be considered without virtue by those who think they know her best. In six words he throws out a line across the deep divide between Jew and Samaritan that few people attempt to bridge.

God is forever the bridge across the chasms of people's own creation. Physically, that woman is at the top of the well but spiritually she is at the bottom and her well is dry. How God loves us! He could justly sit on his throne and chastise us and condemn us, but so great is his love that he comes right down to where we are, our gutter, and offers to lead us out on the path from Hell to Heaven.

Does Jesus sit in the dust merely because he is tired, or is it because he does not want to tower over her and make her feel intimidated and vulnerable that he lowers himself and lets her look down on him?

On meeting this woman, Jesus sees that her mind and eyes are upon wells and water, so that is where he meets her, just where she is. And as we sit and watch we shall see him reveal himself in the world she lives in.

The woman is startled at Christ's request. Not only is she a Samaritan and he a Jew, and they – like oil and water – do not mix or relate to one another, but it was undesirable, unacceptable even, in good Jewish circles for a rabbi ever to converse with a woman.

Jesus, as he often does, defies convention and accepted practice, and the woman retorts, 'You are a Jew!' Whether this was meant to be derogatory, we do not know. If an affront was there Christ sidesteps it, as he does the question she asks. But he doesn't sidestep the issue before them both.

He says, 'If you knew the gift of God and who it is that asks you for a drink...' (v 10). It is so easy to see why she was ignorant of these matters, but do we who claim to know him understand much more? Have we even begun to know what God gives or who it is who speaks to us, asks of us?

The woman's reply only accentuates the divide between them. He is about the fountain of life itself – indeed he is the Fountain of Life itself – and she is about buckets, pitchers and irksome but necessary daily chores. She has not, even from afar off, viewed the plane on which he stands, the plane to which he wishes to draw her.

'Are you greater than our father Jacob?' she asks. He is, yet this is not the issue at hand or the point at which he can reveal that truth to her. One wonders, 'Is that sarcasm in her voice – another affront?' Whatever, Jesus is not concerned; he bears the pain, for he is more concerned about her than himself. He doesn't make an issue of her

115

ignorance either, but persists in manoeuvring the bait on the hook which is so readily drawing this woman closer.

He emphasises again the quality of the water that he has to give and adds that she can have its unending source, too! Again she misses the point. It appears that she is where she was when the conversation commenced. The respective planes on which the woman and Jesus stand still seem poles apart. But Jesus knows, he discerns that, though it has yet to be swallowed, the bait is now in her mouth and she is assessing and questioning its flavour and texture. Even if it is not understood at this stage the message has registered, it is home in the mind, the seed is planted. The Holy Spirit will reveal more when she is ready for the next move.

Jesus leaves this offer with her and asks to meet her husband. She replies that she hasn't got a husband. At this point Jesus lets her know that he already knows about her past and her present relationships and, surely to her surprise (and possibly to ours too) commends her where she might have expected condemnation.

'You are right,' he says (v 17). 'What you have just said is quite true' (*Good News Bible*). In other words, 'You are a truthful woman.' Again another virtue. Jesus is one to seek the smallest speck of gold in the biggest, blackest slag heap. 'A bruised reed he will not break, and a smouldering wick he will not snuff out' (Matthew 12:20).

She is astounded by Jesus' knowledge of her, just as Nathanael was amazed at his knowledge of him a little while earlier (John 1:48, 49). Christ's knowledge of this woman may have been supernatural. Then again we know the Saviour to have been one who always absorbed what was going on around him. He was never so lost in what he was doing or saying as to be insensitive to the reactions and actions around him.

Jesus had a sensitivity and discernment which we would do well to emulate and which the Holy Spirit desires to give to all who would follow him. He would pick up moods and innuendoes and non-verbal cues. Though there is no biblical evidence to help us, it wouldn't surprise me in the least if, when Jesus passed along that self-same road to Jerusalem some time before, he had heard talk of this woman while

116

he was at Sychar. Perhaps, while getting refreshment at that self-same well, he had heard the gossip and had made a point of being there at that time in the hope of meeting the poor woman on his return journey. Either way would be in tune with what we know of Jesus' sensitivity to people and closeness to God.

Scholars tell us it is probable that Sychar is the same as the Arab village of Askar, which is half a mile north of Jacob's Well. It is really strange that Jesus sent his disciples on ahead to get food, only for them to return to him and then retrace their steps afterwards on their journey north. I can't help wondering whether he needed his disciples out of the way for him to reach this woman. Certainly we who claim to love him, indeed do love him after a fashion, are often more of an obstruction than a help to him. And it does appeal to my sense of humour that the disciples, having gone to all that trouble and trudged all the way to the village and back to get that food for Jesus, find on their return that he no longer feels hungry!

The woman is now on the edge of spiritual things and is showing the first signs of thirst and awakening, though her question shows concern for religious practices rather than spiritual realities. But now Jesus can draw her nearer his goal. He takes her from *where* God ought to be worshipped, which was her main concern and the main concern of her contemporaries who believed it to be God's main concern, to *how* he ought to be worshipped – 'in spirit and in truth' (v 24). This is the critical and crucial element both in worship and all our dealings with God. Such is the authority with which he speaks, as she has heard no other rabbi speak, that a thought enters her head. Dare she voice what has suddenly entered her mind? Could it be? No! But...!

'I know that Messiah is coming. When he comes, he will explain everything to us' (v 25). She is ready; she is safely on the line, ready to be reeled in.

'I who speak to you am he.'

Wonder of wonders she, who is the least among the least, arrives at a point in one conversation that it took the searching, listening, seeking disciples half Christ's ministry to arrive at. Though her faith is only half-faith and her knowledge of the Saviour hardly even rudimentary, she is on Christ's plane at last. The barrier of her past sin has been revealed and cast away, allowing the Holy Spirit to transport her into a world she could never have imagined before.

As we watch the disciples return we cannot help but smile at the bemused expressions on their faces at the sight of this now joyous woman speaking with Jesus. One doesn't have to look too deeply into the face of a woman such as this to see her past in her eyes, in her mouth, in those lines that speak so clearly. They can see what she is (or rather was), and they are thinking, and they are wondering, but not one of them – not even Peter – says a word.

As the woman leaves Jesus' company and makes for home, Jesus turns his attention to his disciples. When they left him he was weary and hungry. Now he is refreshed and the tiredness has gone. Here was a practical illustration of what the prophet of old said, 'He gives strength to the weary and increases the power of the weak. Even youths grow tired and weary, and young men stumble and fall; but those who hope in the Lord will renew their strength' (Isaiah 40:29-31). Such was his delight in and appetite for his Father's work that he had little appetite for the food they had for him.

Often our appetite is more for the carnal than the spiritual, more for the things of this world that never satisfy, rather than the things of Heaven that would have our cup running over. His disciples are concerned for him, they express their anxiety, they implore him to eat. He says he has eaten already, food they know nothing of – yet. They wonder who the secret benefactor is. 'This may be said of all good Christians too, that they have meat to eat that others know not of: joy with which a stranger does not intermeddle (relate)' (Matthew Henry).

Jesus then makes it clear to his disciples that he has been harvesting and that harvesting is pressing work, urgent work – not something to be put off, to be done eventually, when all is favourable, in four months time, but now. By his example, we see that it is not to be postponed just because we are weary or hungry or perhaps not in the mood.

It is rewarding work. Jesus says, 'Even now the reaper draws his wages, even now he harvests the crop for eternal life, so that the sower and the reaper may be glad together' (v 36). Although there is an eternal reward awaiting those who do as God would have them do, the reaper does receive a reward now. Jesus was rewarded, filled and refreshed as he drew the woman to himself. And the sowers, who see nothing for their labours – a sown field looks exactly the same the day after it is sown as it did the day before – celebrate with the reaper. They rejoice at the results of what was their hard work too. There are many sowers who go to Heaven having faithfully sowed good seeds in good ground and done a solid work, yet die seeing no fruit for their labours. How they must be jumping up and down with joy in the royal box, in the heavenly arena, at sight of the reaper (who possibly never even knew them) harvesting what they sowed.

It is relatively easy work. Frequently someone else has done the sowing or planting and maybe yet another all the watering (1 Corinthians 3:6-9) and God has ripened the fruit and prepared the harvest. Real sowing is hard work, and can be soul-destroying work, lonely work. A sower is up before dawn, when the weather is often bitterly cold and/or wet. He trudges the field and often weeps with the frost biting his fingers.

How different for the reaper. It's summertime, warm and inviting, he either takes his scythe to the field or his ladder to the tree and, despite the disappointments and failures, he will often see the results of his labours. It is hard work, but it is relatively easy compared to that of sowing. The sowing is often done with tears, while the reaping is always done with joy (Psalm 126:5). As Jesus told his disciples, 'I sent you to reap what you have not worked for. Others have done the hard work, and you have reaped the benefits of their labour' (v 38). The Old Testament prophets sowed seeds, many of them sowed with tears. Yet if it were not for them the woman could not have said, 'I know that Messiah is coming' (v 25).

Before we get to creep away, notice the pitcher still residing where the woman put it – empty (v 28)! We aren't the only ones to see it. At least one disciple noticed it and thought sufficient of that tiny thing

119

to record it. So – what about the water? Always, to those who find Christ, that which at one time seemed so important, so necessary and indispensable becomes an incidental, while that which was previously not even considered becomes our all in all.

Hold on! What is that coming up the road? It's that woman leading a crowd. She has told them of what she has found and they want to discover this Jesus for themselves. Never underestimate the value of sharing the message with one person, concentrating all your effort, attention and encouragement on one individual. One never knows where God will send the ripples when you throw just one stone into a pool.

A woman pleaded to God for her son and the results of that prayer are still reverberating around the great nation of China. Her son's name? James Hudson Taylor.

Albert McMakin cared about a young teenager who had no interest in spiritual matters. When an evangelist visited his local town the youngster rejected Albert's invitations to attend. Although discouraged, Albert wouldn't give up. He owned a truck and offered his 16-year-old young friend the powerful incentive of driving it to the meeting. That did it. Billy drove a truck full of young people to the meeting and was captivated by what he heard there. It completely changed his life. Albert helped harvest one who then reached millions. His name? Billy Graham. It is said that Billy Graham has spoken about Jesus, live, to more people than anyone else in history – more than 200 million people. Don't underestimate the importance of winning one, you may be God's key to opening a floodgate.

When Jesus told his disciples that the fields were ripe for harvest (v 35), they must have wondered what evidence there was for his statement, his discourse had been with one solitary soul. Stand and watch their faces now as the woman returns like the Pied Piper with a crowd in her wake.

I want to encourage you who are ministers with small congregations that may seem unresponsive to your earnest longings, don't let your senses deceive you, there may well be far more going on than you realise.

After years of service in South Africa, the famous missionary Robert Moffat returned to Scotland to recruit helpers. When he arrived one cold, wintry night at the church where he was to speak, he was dismayed that only a small group had come out to hear him. What bothered him even more was that the only people there were women. He was grateful for their interest, but he had hoped to challenge men; he had even chosen as his text, 'Unto you, O men, I call' (Proverbs 8:4 *King James Version*).

In his discouragement he almost failed to notice the 'wee' boy in the loft pumping the bellows of the organ. Moffat felt frustrated as he gave the message, for he realised that very few women could be expected to undergo the rigorous life in undeveloped jungles. But God was about his business in that place, and there was a harvest that Moffat knew nothing of at the time, for no one had visibly volunteered that night in response to his call.

That young boy assisting the organist was deeply moved by the challenge and, as a result, he promised God there and then that he would follow in the footsteps of this pioneer missionary. And he remained true to his vow. When he grew up, he went and ministered to the unreached tribes of Africa. His name? David Livingstone! Moffat never ceased to wonder that the appeal which he had intended for men had stirred a young boy who eventually became a mighty power for God.

'Did you notice,' asks a friend, 'that Jesus' disciples came back from the village they went to with only "sandwiches", while she returned from her village with a crowd of seekers?'

'No, it hadn't dawned on me,' I reply. 'But isn't it strange that she, who has only just encountered Jesus, is unable to stop talking about him, while they who have been with him and known him some time…?'

As we now make our delayed departure from beneath the shade of the tree, aware that in response to the crowd's request Jesus is going to stay a further two days, we realise that we have hardly begun to draw from the well of beauty and truth that we have just witnessed in this brief encounter with the Teacher. I am certain that John, the recorder of this incident, might well have commented on this one incident, as he did on the rest of Christ's life and ministry, that if all the truths about Jesus that are hidden in this story were written down one by one, the whole world could not hold the books that would be written (see John 21:25).

Chapter 17

The Fields Are Ripe

When the disciples returned from the town with food for Jesus and the woman left his company, Jesus turned to his disciples and said, 'I tell you, open your eyes and look at the fields! They are ripe for harvest' (John 4:35). This verse troubled me for years, especially the phrase, 'They are ripe for harvest.' Trying to avoid the point of my personal discomfort, I sought relief in other translations, but in none was there a solace. Jesus quite clearly states that there is fruit ready to be picked, and he makes this statement amid the scepticism around him which said the harvest was yet to come, that things were not yet ready. 'Do you not say,' says Jesus, '"Four months more and then the harvest"?' It is neither his saying nor his belief.

If we have genuinely endeavoured to lead men and women to Christ, only to be met time and time again with abysmal failure or extremely limited success, we have a tendency, having reached the end of our resources of imagination, ingenuity and energy, to seek refuge from our self-condemnation, guilt and failure by telling ourselves that we are just sowers not reapers. We say that the age of harvests is an age past never to return, or an age yet to come. Or we say that the gospel cannot penetrate the rationale or the mindset of this present age, this postmodern, post-Christendom age.

We read the words of Jesus in Matthew 13:14, 15, as he quotes Isaiah, 'You will be ever hearing but never understanding; you will be ever seeing but never perceiving. For this people's heart has become calloused; they hardly hear with their ears, and they have closed their eyes. Otherwise they might see with their eyes, hear with their ears, understand with their hearts and turn, and I would heal them.'

123

'That is why we do not harvest,' we say. 'The people have defective sight and hearing!' And we back up this line of thought with a host of other scriptural recalls. Yet still our rest is incomplete. We remain uncomfortable, for we know that, despite the fact that thorn bushes, hard paths and rocky ground may predominate, good soil there will be and sufficient good soil, according to Jesus, for there to be an abundant harvest (Mark 4:1-9, 13-20). In a world of deafness there are those ready to hear. In a world of blindness there are those ready to see.

So where lies the fault? Let us change the metaphor. In Luke 5:2 we read of how the fishermen, soon to be Jesus' disciples, had given up fishing because they had failed to catch anything. They had pulled their boats up out of the water and left them and were busying themselves washing their nets, resigned to the fact that they had failed.

Was it because there were no fish to be caught? Was it because the fish were uncatchable? According to the verses that follow, neither of these was the cause of their abysmal failure. Nor was the reason a lack of effort or laziness. With all their energy, time and expertise, Simon and his companions had failed to catch one solitary fish. As Simon says, 'Master, we've worked hard all night and haven't caught anything' (v 5).

These men were not lazy. They had worked all night long, no doubt trying every conceivable technique they had, pooling all their knowledge and experience, yet they had failed. Even now they were not idle, they were washing their nets – a necessary chore for any fisherman. But this chore, however necessary, would not catch them any fish. They were no longer fishing.

We can't help feeling for them. They are so much like us. Having failed to catch fish for the Kingdom, we frequently give up and just do something closely aligned to it, something necessary even, but something that is not fishing. We assure ourselves that we are 'being faithful', 'holding on'; that 'being an influence' is sufficient; that any results are in God's hands.

Some of us will have smiled at that cartoon of a fisherman in the middle of a river in his waders, with line cast and net handy, being asked if he had caught any fish. He responds by saying that he hasn't caught any, but that he has influenced quite a few.

'It is his work not ours,' we say. 'In four months time,' we say. 'When the Church has made the changes it needs to make,' we say. Meanwhile we play at evangelism and attribute our lack of results to the non-receptiveness of the world that we live in.

We invite folk to meetings and poke leaflets through letter boxes. Some of us conduct meetings in the street, offending a few, blessing some. We busy ourselves with good works, remembering how Jesus spoke of men seeing our good works and glorifying our Father in Heaven (Matthew 5:16), and fail either to see or to acknowledge that most of the glory and gratitude falls on us rather than him. Satan, the father of lies, can use the truth very subtly to convince or confuse the less discerning. He backs up his deceit with plausible reasoning and even biblical support. Of course Jesus commended 'good works' – the cup of water (Matthew 10:42), visiting the prisoner, feeding the hungry, clothing the naked (Matthew 25:34-46). Of course nets need washing – nothing will be caught if they are not maintained. The cleverness of Satan's subtle deception is that he would make it appear that we are taking issue with the dictates of Christ himself.

We can do all these things – many do – and still miss the very core of the gospel, the central purpose of Christ: to seek the lost (Matthew 18:12), to save sinners (1 Timothy 1:15). The central issue is the eternal issue. As important as a person's present state is, as a person's present welfare is, it is not the most important thing. What matters more than anything is a person's relationship with God and where he or she will spend eternity. The Church needs to major in on this again.

The great 19th-century evangelist, D. L. Moody, used to say, 'The main thing is to keep the main thing the main thing.' I would suggest that we need to *make* the main thing the main thing again. If our boats are now out of the water and the souls of men are no longer our immediate or ultimate concern, then all our commendable works that ought to result from an earnest desire to save the lost become merely the substitute for it.

I often think that this life is like a waiting room for Hell for those who do not know Jesus. Where the waiting room is an uncomfortable, dirty or unpleasant place, we Christians go in and decorate it. We put in carpet, running water, heating, new furnishings and other pleasantnesses to keep the occupants comfortable, amused and occupied while they wait. Most times they are grateful and appreciative. But it is still Hell's waiting room. It is somewhere that those within its confines need to be rescued from. Provide for the needy, the hungry, the lonely, the dispossessed and the damaged by all means. We should. We must. But above all else we need to be focused on getting them out of that waiting-room-for-Hell by any means possible and on to the road with Jesus to Heaven.

Dr Edward Jenner, that great physician who discovered the vaccine for smallpox, was introduced to a friend by a well-known minister, Sir Rowland Hill, as having saved more lives than any other man. Dr Jenner's reply was, 'You said I saved more lives than any other man, and that may be true. However, I would rather have it said of me as it might be said of you, that I saved more souls!'

Catherine Booth it was who, shortly before her death in 1890, said, 'I can remember a sort of inward pity for what I thought then was the small expectations of the Church... I can remember how disappointed I felt at the comparatively small results which seemed to give satisfaction.'

Chapter 18

The Main Thing

In the early days of The Salvation Army, back in East London, leaders were referred to as 'evangelists', and that, indeed, was their role: to reach and lead the lost to Christ. Many confined themselves to evangelism and nothing else, so that the problem was not that of getting people saved, but rather what to do with them afterwards. Social work and the relief of physical and material deprivation was often a part of the work of salvation, but always in the minds of those dealing with the immediate wellbeing of a convert was concern for his or her ultimate wellbeing. Even in 1866 (pre-Salvation Army days), with a cholera epidemic, continued unemployment and its intense accompanying distress, William Booth and his workers kept their heads and did not allow themselves to be stampeded either into distributing food, clothing, blankets, etc, indiscriminately, or losing sight of the Christian Mission's first objective, that of the eternal salvation of the people.

Even the extensive organisation of this growing Movement did not impede the evangelist. Rather, it provided a means of retaining and channelling new converts, a problem that few of the missions of that time had resolved. The evangelist continued to concentrate on reaching the lost, the Mission's priority. Though the discipling and care of converts were very important, the priority was always that of getting more of the unsaved saved. When a person got saved they were immediately discipled, mobilised and encouraged to get their friends and families saved. Taking his son to an unsavoury, smoke-filled public house, William Booth said to young Bramwell, 'Willie, these are our people; these are the people I want you to live for and bring to Christ.' Obviously a word from a God-fearing father to his son, but surely as we look at the eternal state of those around us who live without Christ, is it not a word from God to us all?

One thing I think is true of most of the Church in this country, its emphasis on eternal issues has changed/moved. The thing that was, at one time, the main thing of the Church is no longer the main thing anymore. There are a number of reasons for this.

1. Churches are too busy doing 'churchy things' with the limited resources of money and manpower they have.

2. They are more concerned about maintaining the institution than being mobilised for mission. Often more time and energy is spent on maintaining some outdated delivery vehicle than the thing that the Church was created to deliver.

3. It is easier to see and then respond to a person's physical and material needs than their spiritual need.

4. Confidence has been lost:

   a) Confidence in the Bible as the word of God.

   b) Confidence in the truths of God's righteousness, the seriousness of sin and God's wrath and judgment.

   c) Confidence in God's longing for, and power to penetrate hearts and save the lost.

This process of moving away from the 'main thing' began over 100 years ago. In his lecture entitled *Why Did The English Stop Going To Church?*, based on in-depth research, Dr Michael Watts stated that the highest recorded voluntary[2] church attendance in England was that recorded in a census taken on Sunday 30 March 1851, when almost 40% of the population attended Sunday worship. He discovered that this was as a result of the education provided for children by the Church of England and the subsequent evangelism carried out by the Nonconformists when that generation reached adulthood.

An analysis that Dr Watts made of the conversion experiences of 670 Nonconformists who claimed to have been converted between

[2] Prior to the 19th century the majority of English men and women were reluctant to attend worship. The only thing that could induce them to worship regularly was the threat of fines or imprisonment. Admittedly, there would still be those who attended worship in deference, to please to their landlord or employer, but the vast majority of those in the 1851 census attended of their own free will.

1780 and 1850 revealed that over one third had been brought up as Anglicans and were taught in their childhood that everyone had 'sinned and come short of the glory of God' and deserved to be punished with eternal damnation for breaking God's moral code.

Dr Watts concluded, 'It was left to the Evangelicals to point out that Hell could be avoided by accepting, through faith, the sacrifice that Christ had made for sinners at Calvary.' From his analysis, Dr Watts discovered that it was that 'fear of death, fear of judgment, fear above all of the eternal torment in the fires of Hell' that was the major factor that caused those 670 to consider and then respond to the evangelists' message.

To discover exactly when and why the decline set in, Dr Watts then carried out detailed research of denominational records and other sources, ensuring that he was comparing like with like, as there was not a similar universal church census for quite a number of decades. He discovered that the maintenance of the high attendance of Sunday worship for more than 30 years following the 1851 census was mainly due to the reawakening that began in 1859, and that the decline began in the mid-1880s.

So what caused the present decline which started all those years ago? Some people have suggested that the shadow cast by Charles Darwin's *On The Origin Of Species* was the cause, others, the flowering of British science, while still others proposed that it was German biblical criticism, or a combination of all three. But while these may have blunted the churches' message, they were not, as we might have expected, the main concern of the churches back then. According to the religious press of the 1860s and 1870s, the far more worrying cause of concern seems to have been the 'reinterpreting if not rejecting of the orthodox doctrine of future punishment'. Certainly those churchmen who resisted this change in the doctrinal stance of many clergy at that time saw it as the most dangerous threat to the Church's progress.

Although the conviction that those without Christ would spend eternity in Hell was a major factor in people being converted in the first part of the century, by the latter part many Christians regarded the doctrine with distaste. When F. W. Farrar published *Eternal Hope,* in which he rejected the idea of an eternal punishment, he received many letters stating that the reason so many working men rejected Christianity was because it held on to the belief in the 'everlasting damnation of the overwhelming majority of mankind'.

What then followed was that clergy shifted in their view and their preaching, from a focus on the eternal destinies of the saved and unsaved to focusing on an improved life here on earth in an effort to present a more attractive, acceptable, amenable and tasteful message to the non-Christian. However, instead of churches seeing their congregations increase, this change of emphasis saw the gradual erosion of their numbers. Dr Watts remarked, 'Liberal Christianity did not fill the churches, it helped empty them.' In focusing on offering commodities such as 'fellowship, entertainment and knowledge', as George La Noue and Dean Kelley put it, they offered no more than many a secular agency, while doing away with the one incentive that Christ gave to his Church: salvation, the promise of eternal life and a supernatural life after death.

Charles Spurgeon, the great Baptist preacher, was very concerned that the orthodox faith was being eroded or 'downgraded', with the truths of the atonement and eternal punishment being rejected. He believed that it would lead to the decline of the Church. This had an historical precedence. In the previous century a similar liberalisation of the English Presbyterians had taken place which had led to their decline.

Spurgeon's stand, which began in 1887, resulted in his resignation from the Baptist Union. He and his ilk, with their continued emphasis on the eternal punishment of the unsaved, became an embarrassment to those who embraced the new thinking. William Booth must have been aware of the change taking place in the doctrine of the Church around him for, when asked by an American newspaper at the dawn of the 20th century what he saw to be the chief danger of the coming century, his reply was, 'In answer to your enquiry, I consider that the chief dangers which confront the coming century will be religion without the Holy Ghost; Christianity without Christ; forgiveness without repentance; salvation without regeneration; politics without God; and Heaven without Hell.'

It seems logical to me that if there is not an eternal punishment for sin, then sin is not as serious, obnoxious and repulsive to God as the Bible says it is and, consequently, God's wrath would appear irrational, unreasonable and unjust. If there is no eternal punishment, why did God need to go to such enormous lengths at such enormous cost to save us from such a non-existent punishment? In short, why would people need a Saviour if there is nothing, other than their ills in this short life, to save them from? If God is indeed God, would he have even contemplated the total humiliation of himself that entering human flesh entailed, never mind the rest, unless both the result of our sin and the enormity of his love and heartache for us all were not so great?

If we were but closer to him we would know the truth and we would share his burden, see the issues from his viewpoint and realise that the Bible and what Christ had to say on the subject of sin and punishment there is true. Yes, there are things that we don't understand, things that are difficult to digest. That is nothing new. We in this enlightened, more knowledgeable, scientific age are not the first to see difficulties or unanswerable questions. But, as with our forefathers, it need not prevent us from regaining confidence in the fact that the Bible does not *contain* the word of God, it *is* the word of God.

While academics theorise as to what is myth, fact or mere parable in the Bible, we must hold solidly to the truth we claim, which is that God himself brought together the Bible in the form we have it, to be accepted as his word. Aware of this continuing debate, William Booth himself said it was to be treated as 'the only authorised and trustworthy revelation of the mind of God' (*The Bible, Its Divine Revelation, Inspiration And Authority*).

The truth is that often theories treated as fact in one generation are discarded like a fashion garment by a later one. The fact is that God himself has done and still does extraordinary things, supernatural things through his word, the Bible. He transforms minds and hearts and lives and even whole communities through the reading of it, the exposition of it and obedience to its teaching. God himself confirms that it has his approval and bears his authority by what he does when it is accepted as his word.

Also, when we came to know God himself through Jesus, we recognised the God of our experience in the God of the Bible and it came alive. What previously may have been dull and boring became exciting to read. Has there ever been another book that has done and can do what this book can do?

When Susan Budd analysed the experiences of 150 secularists who rejected Christianity between 1850 and 1950 she found the crucial factor leading men and women in her sample to renounce Christianity was a conviction that what the churches taught was morally wrong, ie, eternal punishment, Hell, the Atonement and damnation for unbelievers.

So what are we to do with regard to those who find the message unacceptable, unpalatable, repugnant? Alter the truth because it does not suit or fit a person's concept of the issues? Trying to ingratiate ourselves with the world and its view has done the gospel no favours. In trying to make Christianity more relevant to men and women of the modern world, the Church has actually made itself irrelevant. The history of Christianity and the Bible tells us that the soul-saving gospel message has always been both a stumbling block and foolishness to many. It has always been distasteful and an offence to the majority. It has always provoked hostility and rejection – we only need to look at the Acts of the Apostles and the lives of people like John Wesley to see that. But at one and the same time, where it has been faithfully presented, uncompromised, in all its fullness, God has always responded and blessed it with fruit.

Let us all return with confidence to the Bible as the word of God, God's truth. Let us accept with confidence what it says regarding God's righteousness, the seriousness of sin, God's wrath and judgment and God's merciful remedy provided for saving people from their just deserts. Let us have confidence in God's longing for and power to penetrate hearts and save the lost.

Chapter 19

Partners With God

Whatever our opinion and attitude to harvesting the ripe and ready crop, one thing is certain, and that is that God is already out there in those fields preparing them for harvest. By whatever means the seed may have been sown, whatever the influences that have watered it, the growth and the ripening ready for harvesting is God's work (1 Corinthians 3:6, 7). And it is work which he has been doing since the beginning of time through his Son. In his Gospel, John speaks of the light coming into the world and shining on all humankind (1:9). In 1 John 1:5 we read, 'God is light; in him there is no darkness at all,' and Christ confirms that he is 'the light of the world' (John 8:12). As F. B. Meyer puts it: 'There has never been an age in which the divine light has not shone over our world. Not gospel light, not the light as we have it, but still light. And whatever light existed was due to the presence and the working of the Lord Jesus.'

Since the creation of humankind, God in Christ has shone on, and still shines on all people, revealing himself in a multitude of ways – such as his incredible creativity. As Romans 1:20 puts it, 'For since the creation of the world God's invisible qualities – his eternal power and his divine nature – have been clearly seen, being understood from what has been made, so that men are without excuse.' He revealed and still reveals himself in his goodness that he pours out on everyone, the evil and the good, the righteous and the unrighteous (Matthew 5:45); in the intuitions of truth that we call conscience with its instinctive sense of good and evil (Romans 2:14, 15); and more recently (less than 4,000 years) the Scriptures.

God in Christ has always been reaching out with a yearning to gather his wayward children in his arms. Commenting on Christ's lament over Jerusalem in Luke 13:34, William Barclay says: 'It is quite clear that Jesus could never have spoken like this, unless he had more than once gone with his offer of love to Jerusalem; but in the first three Gospels there is no indication of any such visits.' More visits there definitely were according to John's Gospel. However, I would humbly suggest that Christ's words, 'How often I have longed to gather your children together, as a hen gathers her chicks under her wings, but you were not willing!', might well not have been a reference so much to those visits, but more a reference to his eternal love, a love that existed before his incarnation, a love that existed from before the beginning of time, a love that had witnessed the triumphs, tribulations and tragedies of that city and its people and had always longed for their peace. Christ's words are surely an echo of God's desire to fulfil Psalm 91:4, 'He will cover you with his feathers, and under his wings you will find refuge.'

When Christ became man, that light which had always shone on all people, previously only vaguely perceived, was seen clearly, in the flesh, dwelling among us – standing before our very eyes. We beheld the Father's glory in his Son. And today, that self-same eternal light continues to shine on all humankind, but now it is light given clarity in the form of the person Jesus, clarity enhanced by the Holy Spirit when he dwells in the heart of a believer. That which God has been endeavouring to reveal to people through his eternal light shining on them, the Holy Spirit makes clear in the life and ministry and person of Jesus.

There are those who sense that eternal light – those who are aware of 'something', even if they can't explain it or understand it – and those who don't, who sense nothing at all. Though Christ was always in the world, and though God made the world through him, the world did not recognise him (John 1:10). There are those who have experienced something of the light's rays, known something of its characteristic warmth, purity, comfort, strength, gentleness and/or other revealing qualities, and yet do not know what 'it' is that they have sensed or where it comes from.

A large proportion of non-Christians have sensed that all-pervading, seeking light in one or more of a multiplicity of ways, but do not recognise 'him' for who he is. They have had a sense of comfort when no human agent has been near. They have received strength and wondered where it came from. Is it little wonder to us that Sir Alister Hardy, founder of the Religious Experience Research Unit at Oxford, who conducted extensive research into people's beliefs and attitudes, discovered that a very large number of people do experience what he describes as a sense of a higher benevolent power? They sense it in a number of ways, such as being guided, comforted, challenged or given strength.

The wise Christian worker meeting such people will do well to follow the example of St Paul when he met with the Athenians and identify and then tune in to and build on what God has already done. The Athenians on Mars Hill were aware of this light that shines on all humankind shining on them, this 'benevolent power' as Sir Alister Hardy describes it. They were aware that there was a god beyond their previously limited concepts, a god who could not be contained in an idol of silver or gold or wood, a god who was invisible, a god whom they did not know. Paul was thus able to declare, 'Now what you worship as something unknown I am going to proclaim to you' (Acts 17:23), adding a rider in verse 27, 'He is not far from each one of us.' He related their previous experience to the reality of what the one true God was like and what he had done in Jesus, and when St Paul introduced them to Jesus many (not all) did recognise him.

What we find when such a person seeks and finds Christ as Lord and Saviour is that so many previous experiences they had of God reaching out to them suddenly become clear, even though they failed to recognise them for what they were at the time. Before coming to Christ they were like the partially sighted man who, when asked by Jesus, 'Do you see anything?' answered, 'I see people; they look like trees walking around' (Mark 8:23, 24). Often such a new-born Christian will say that God had always been speaking to him/her, trying to reach him/her, but only on meeting with Jesus did it become obvious what had previously been going on.

On the other hand, those who have never sensed God's light shining on them are like someone completely blind. They are particularly hard work. Their minds are often closed. They are blind. If a man is blind he will not see what is in front of his nose, however clear it is. The partially sighted need a miracle, the blind need an even bigger one.

During the Christmas season of 1879 an agnostic reporter in Boston, USA, was wanting to write an original story about Christmas for his newspaper, but as hard as he tried to think of one, no idea was forthcoming. Walking home through the snow from his office one evening he saw three little girls standing in front of a store window full of toys. Two of them were excitedly talking to the third in a most demonstrative manner, while she stood motionless, listening. Curious, the reporter walked closer to find out what was going on and, eavesdropping on their conversation, discovered that the third girl was blind and the other two girls were doing their best to describe to her the toys that they could see. He had never considered how difficult it was to explain to someone without sight what something looks like. That incident became the basis of his newspaper story.

Two weeks later the great evangelist Dwight L. Moody was conducting a meeting in the city and the reporter decided to attend. His purpose was to discover and report some inconsistency in the evangelist. Imagine his surprise when Moody used his Christmas newspaper story about the children to illustrate a truth. 'Just as the blind girl couldn't visualise the toys,' said Moody, 'so an unsaved person can never see Christ.' The line of thought that began as a result of hearing Moody's message resulted in the reporter seeking and finding Christ, in him experiencing the miracle of sight to the blind.

Blind or partially sighted, whichever the case, one thing we can be sure of is that, in any given encounter with another person, God has already been at work before we arrive on the scene, whether or not he or she has sensed it. Even if an individual neither recognises the light nor acknowledges it, or indeed denies the light in his/her life, it *has* shone on him/her. God doesn't wait for us to move before he does. He is indeed the Good Shepherd. In one or more of many ways individuals will have often perceived 'something,' and some of those people will be ripe or near-ripe for harvest.

In the Old Testament we have a picture of a God who goes ahead of his people and prepares a situation for them before they arrive there. In Exodus 13:21 and 22 we read that during the day the Lord went in front of them in a pillar of cloud to show them the way, and during the night he went before them in a pillar of fire to give them light. He was always ahead of his people. Our God always prepares our path. He prepared the widow of Zarephath for Elijah (1 Kings 17:9). The ministry of all the prophets and all the Scriptures of the Old Testament (Luke 24:27), together with the work of John the Baptist (John 1:6, 7), were all God's preparation for Christ's ministry. God has already done a work and prepared the way for us to minister to many an unsaved person and to reap a harvest.

Though a person might be a complete stranger to us he/she is not a complete stranger to God. As we have already said, God has already been at work in him/her, whether he/she is aware of anything or not. And despite the immediate and apparent reasons that may have brought us together, God in his great wisdom and mercy may well have engineered the encounter so that something of eternal significance might take place. Many of the stories in this book are a confirmation of this. The knowledge that God is already at work in the life of an individual, and that there is possible fruit to be picked, should encourage every Christian to be permanently taking a good look at the fields he/she find himself/herself in. In any situation, with any group or individual, we should be asking ourselves, is there a reason that perhaps I cannot see as to why God would have me here?

In our day-to-day ordinary encounters, at the bus stop, in the bank queue, at the supermarket checkout, in our work or in our leisure, we who are God's people, indeed his agents, should be focused on those around us, observing and analysing and seeking what is on God's mind regarding the people we meet. While other people may be preoccupied with themselves, their own lives, interests and problems, our focus, like that of Jesus, should be on others. Often, if we ask questions, not only does the stranger sense our genuine interest in and concern for him/her, but we also discover something of what is going on in the other person and what God wants us to hear. What a thrill it is to discover that it is indeed a divine appointment that God made for us; and what an equal thrill it is to discover that this time we didn't miss it. I sometimes wonder just how many I miss, which makes me wonder just how many thousands of divine appointments God makes on a daily basis between Christians and non-Christians that are missed.

Certainly, if we were more tuned into what God is already doing in the lives of those around us we might be less clumsy in our evangelism. Sometimes we think that people have rejected Christ, rejected the gospel, when the truth is that often they have reacted negatively to our assault on their ears or our insensitivity to their sensibilities. God doesn't want elephants in the woods gathering bluebells. Not only will we return with nothing, but the bluebells we leave behind, that were so ready for the gatherers' gentle touch, will be in no condition to be gathered in the future by anyone, however delicate their touch, however sensitive they may be.

How often, for instance, has the Bible been used as a bludgeon on a poor soul, or as a vehicle to show off an unchallengable, superior knowledge? It is a great tool, our number one resource but, as any master craftsman will tell you, a tool has to be handled correctly. As nourishing as a loaf of bread might be, and as hungry as a pigeon might be, who would throw a loaf of bread at a hungry pigeon and then blame the pigeon for flying off or for being hurt should the loaf and the poor bird make contact? That poor pigeon might never trust anyone carrying a loaf of bread again – and who could blame it? In that poor creature's eyes, bread would always represent a missile rather than a morsel.

However, don't let us criticise the enthusiast for his/her enthusiasm. Better a misguided enthusiast who is teachable than someone who lacks enthusiasm and has no care for the lost. At least that enthusiasm can be redirected.

As a gunman aims at the heart of his victim, we need to seek out and aim our attentions at the heart of the person's (albeit unconscious) encounter with the light. People are all different. They are individuals, each at a different stage spiritually. There is soil where no seed has germinated and other soil where it has. There is the fruit tree with no fruit as yet, and there is the fruit tree with an abundance, some ripe and ready for harvesting, some not quite ready.

We are partners with God, junior partners at that, and we must seek his guidance, ask for discernment as to where those we meet are spiritually and what he would have us do, and should there be fruit waiting to be picked, how it might be best picked successfully.

As a naughty boy I remember throwing a cricket bat into a farmer's apple tree because I fancied one of his apples. Though eventually I got myself one, it wasn't a very good idea – not only was my prize apple damaged but the fruit left behind on the tree was damaged too. Fruit is delicate and needs to be handled with care. Whereas a sickle may be appropriate for a cornfield, most times fruit is picked individually.

Lord, give us all discernment, give us sensitivity, that each of us, like Ananias, might listen to and learn from Christ what has already been done in the life of those we meet (Acts 9:10-19), that we might sensitively and delicately identify and pick the fruit that he has prepared and placed before us.

Chapter 20

No Cause For Pride

In 1997 many people in Britain were introduced to the words STANDING ON THE SHOULDERS OF GIANTS on the edge of the £2 coin. It was a quotation that Sir Isaac Newton made in a letter to his fellow scientist Robert Hooke in 1676, where he modestly claimed that his success had been built on the achievements of others. 'If I have seen further,' he wrote, 'it is by standing on the shoulders of giants.' He recognised that he could not have done what he had done without Galileo's and Kepler's work in the fields of physics and astronomy.

But Newton wasn't the first to use the expression 'standing on the shoulders of giants'. In 1159 John of Salisbury wrote in his *Metalogican*: 'Bernard of Chartres used to say, "We are like dwarfs on the shoulders of giants, so that we see more than they, and things at a greater distance, not by virtue of any sharpness of sight on our part, or any physical distinction, but because we are carried high and raised up by their giant size."'

Surely these words were the inspiration for the stained glass window in Chartres Cathedral's south transept, created during the following century. Under the rose window there are five long windows, four of which show the major Old Testament prophets, Isaiah, Jeremiah, Ezekiel and Daniel as gigantic figures with the four New Testament evangelists, Matthew, Mark, Luke and John, much smaller, sitting on their shoulders. The evangelists, though shorter, 'saw more' than the taller Old Testament prophets saw. They saw the Messiah. The prophets spoke of him but never saw him. Yet without the prophets setting the scene for them, the evangelists would never have been able to see what they saw.

So it is with harvesters/reapers. As Jesus said, 'The saying "One sows and another reaps" is true. I sent you to reap what you have not worked for. Others have done the hard work, and you have reaped the benefit of their labour' (John 4:37, 38). What humility Jesus shows. He had just picked that ripe and ready fruit that he met in the person of the woman at the well in Samaria (see chapter 4) with skill and sensitivity, yet he does not take the credit for his superb example of reaping. He acknowledged that seeds were already in there growing, that the fruit was ripe and ready when he met the woman. He acknowledged that preparatory work had already been done by others before he ever arrived on the scene. Someone or maybe many people between them had told her about Jacob and her forefathers. Someone had told her about the Messiah. 'I know that Messiah is coming,' she said. 'When he comes, he will explain everything to us' (v 25).

In every case, without exception, where I have had the privilege of reaping – including the examples I have recorded here – I have discovered that a work has inevitably already been done in the heart of that individual long before my arrival on the scene.

Sometimes it has been a direct work of the Holy Spirit, seemingly unconnected to any human agency, as with a woman who, one Easter Sunday morning having given her family their breakfast, suddenly felt the compulsion to go to church. She hurried and dressed, arriving late for our Salvation Army meeting, but in time for the message. As she listened, the preacher spoke directly into her situation in such a way that she could not believe that the message could have been meant or prepared for anybody other than herself in that crowded hall. It played on her mind all week, so much so she came back the following Sunday and again, with an entirely different message, the same thing happened. She was convinced that God was speaking personally to her, so that when an appeal was made to respond to God's offer of salvation in Jesus and to find in him the answer to her deep need, she did.

At other times, it is a series of influences involving a number of people – the work of faithful sowing, watering and fertilising, often over many years. Some of it will have been hard graft, soul-destroying work, like trying to break up rock-hard soil.

Then there are times when it is gentle, effortless watering: the kindliness of a concerned soul; the atmosphere a Christian brings into a room whenever he/she enters it; the sense of genuine love of Christians towards one another; the example of someone who suffers and even dies in a Christlike way.

The reaper has no cause for pride; God has put everything in place for him/her to do his/her particular work. God is the only one who deserves credit, deserves glory. The Lord of the harvest it is who presides over, co-ordinates, orchestrates and directs the work. Some of the sowers and waterers may no longer be in the field when the crop they worked so hard for and lived for is harvested. Often only God will ever be aware of and able to relate the harvest gathered to those who laboured years or decades before. Among this band of unknown faithful workers will be many a spiritual giant when compared with this dwarf God sent to reap the ripe and ready fruit.

In the story of Cornelius's conversion (Acts 10), someone or, more probably, several people must have sown the seeds and done groundwork in the heart of this centurion years before Peter ever heard of him. He was a God-fearer, one who had separated himself from the pagan worship of his fellow Romans. He was a man given to charity and a man of prayer. He might not have known the God to whom he prayed, but he had responded to the light he had perceived and lived close to God. And as he sought God, God sought him, sending him an angel. Consequently, when Peter was sent to reap the ripe and ready fruit, he was amazed at the ready response to his message.

Philip must have wondered what he was doing on the road to Gaza, having left a revival in Samaria, a fruitful, flourishing ministry, for a desert road (Acts 8:26-38). It wasn't a small thing a few miles away. He was required to travel between 50 and 100 miles along a desert road on foot. How easy it would have been for him to have stayed where he was, where the blessings that he was so enjoying were. Often Christians seek blessings rather than obedience. But Philip was truly a man of God and consequently he did as he was told, even if he had uncertainties and misgivings as to where it might take him.

143

We don't know how many days he trekked along that dry and dusty road or how many travellers and traders he met along the way. We don't know how lonely he now felt, the questions he asked himself, the doubts that entered his head. He must have wondered what it was all about and whether he had got it right. When we live or endeavour to live close to God and he prompts or leads us to go in a certain direction, frequently we have no idea where we are going or where it will lead, or why we are where we are. As you can see from some of the preceding stories, that is often my experience. But it is a case of trusting that God knows what he is about, that he doesn't make mistakes and that he will reveal what he wants to reveal when he is ready, when it is right.

Then, the particular traveller that God had earmarked came by in his chariot and the Holy Spirit told Philip that he was the one he was there for. Prompted to go up and keep close to the chariot, Philip did so and listened. The key to everything is listening – listening to God and listening to the person who is sharing where he/she is. And as he did so he heard familiar words being read from the prophet Isaiah. God's timing was impeccable. Not only was the eunuch reading aloud from the book of Isaiah, but he was reading the very passage that foretold the sufferings of Jesus. How's that for timing? Who had planted the seeds in that man's heart and caused him to read his Bible in the first place? Who knows? Who had influenced, helped and watered that first work? We have no idea. But what is clear is that he was hungry to know more and was ripe and ready for reaping.

This book is a call and an encouragement to reap the harvest that is ripe and ready to be reaped. That is not to dismiss the work of sowing. I've said little about sowing, but, sadly, there is little active sowing in the Church today. Few are the churches where the truths of the gospel message, the facts of eternity, humankind's sinful condition, Heaven and Hell as clearly expressed in the Bible and God's great merciful saving grace as revealed in Jesus are actually presented.

I have met many regular churchgoers who have never had the clear gospel message presented to them. So it is hardly surprising that, too frequently, people within the Church fail to see the need or urgency to reach out to those spiritually lost, beyond their building, and present them with the message of salvation. Any sowing that takes place tends to be of a passive nature.

By merely creating a lovely atmosphere in the company we keep, just showing by our attitude, actions and reactions that we have a different value system to that of the society we live in, and doing good, we hope that people will stumble upon the Good News itself, or deduce it for themselves. Certainly all those things stated should prevail in the life of someone who knows and loves Christ, no question. It is good. It is necessary. But is it really enough? If we do not reveal to observers the reason we are how we are, how are they ever to discover the source of our motivation, what it is that makes us so different? If no one actually tells them anything, how are they to discover it?

St Paul restated what the prophet Joel voiced centuries earlier, 'Everyone who calls on the name of the Lord will be saved' (Joel 2:32). He then added, 'How, then, can they call on the one they have not believed in? And how can they believe in the one of whom they have not heard? And how can they hear without someone preaching to them?' (Romans 10:14).

Nevertheless, there is still sowing taking place. God continues sowing. Where the Church has failed, God has still been doing his work and shining his light on every man (John 1:9) and, as Jesus said, the fields are ripe and ready for harvest (John 4:35) and the 'harvest is plentiful' (Matthew 9:37). Many is the man or woman who has had a sense of God who has never heard the gospel message or been near a place of worship.

Jesus wants us to be concerned about bringing home the harvest. He wants us to call on the Lord of the harvest to send forth workers into his harvest field (Matthew 9:38)! If the harvest isn't gathered when it is ripe and ready we all know what happens to the fruit or wheat or other produce. Some people excuse themselves from the work, saying that they do not have the gift of evangelism. When Jesus called the fishermen from Galilee, he said to them, 'I will *make* you fishers of men' (Mark 1:17, italics mine). There is no evidence that they had the gift of evangelism, nor did they know fully what Jesus meant, but they did have a belief in what he could do for them and with them.

The prayer Jesus tells us to make to God is a request for workers – labourers – not skilled men, not artisans, not experts. It must be great to have the gift of evangelism, I am sure. If it can be identified in a congregation it should be, and those with it should be freed from any other responsibility that would prevent them using their gift. But do not limit what you do for the Lord to the gifts you have – or which others think you have. That should not be our guiding principle. It was not the guiding principle of the prophets. Had Moses, Jeremiah or Isaiah merely looked at the gifts and equipment they had for the task (as indeed they did at first), they would never have allowed God to have done through them the great works that he did.

Timothy's role was to teach and nurture the people of God in his charge. The two letters that Paul wrote to him are full of that sort of pastoral advice but, at the end of his final letter, Paul adds, 'Do the work of an evangelist, discharge all the duties of your ministry' (2 Timothy 4:5). There are duties we all have, whatever the gifts we do or don't possess. Nowhere do we read that evangelism was Timothy's gifting.

While all Christians have faith in the Lord Jesus Christ which has been given them by God, few of us possess that gift of special faith, more powerful faith, mentioned in 1 Corinthians 12:9. We shouldn't, however, allow the absence of that special gift to prevent us from operating in the realm of faith, leaving what God would have us do to others whom we judge better qualified for the task.

From my own experience, many a time as someone has stepped out to fulfil a role he/she is totally unqualified for God has temporarily provided the gift needed to accomplish it. It is a little like the River Jordan parting when the priests carrying the Ark of the Covenant stepped into it. They could have sat on the riverbank waiting for the flooding waters to subside and a way through them to appear. They would have waited for ever. But no, the priests were to step into the

146

Jordan and only as they stepped in would the waters part (Joshua 3:15, 16). It was a Salvation Army officer named Kate Lee, nicknamed the Angel Adjutant, whose motto became, 'I can't, but I must.'

The greatest need is not the gift of evangelism but rather a burden for the lost, the situation they are in and the eternal consequences that will result if they are not saved. More precisely, we need Christ's burden for those who are lost. We need the mind of Christ, the Spirit of Christ, the compassion Christ had for others. We need to be looking at everyone we meet with the eyes of Christ. Jesus was always looking outward to others, reading others, because he had a heart that was ever focused on the condition and needs of others. 'When *he* saw the crowds, he had compassion on them, because they were harassed and helpless, like sheep without a shepherd' (Matthew 9:36, italics mine).

How does the crowd affect us? Does it fill us with compassion? The Greek word translated 'compassion' is actually a much stronger word than its translation would imply. It expresses that deep pain of love, that ache that could easily result in tears, that empathy for what others are experiencing. That is the key to reaping. If we have Christ's mind, Christ's outlook, Christ's heartache, we will wrestle and pray and weep before God until, to some degree, he makes us the fishermen he promised. Pray to the Lord of the harvest for workers/labourers as he told us to and we may well discover that we are the ones he calls/provides!

The compassion Jesus had for multitudes he also had for ones and twos. They received no less attention from him than the crowds. We need to wrestle and pray and weep before God asking that he stir the hearts of our friends, family and neighbours towards him. It was that compassion that drove George Müller to his knees in prayer for others.

In a sermon in 1880 he stated the following: 'In November 1844, I began to pray for the conversion of five individuals. I prayed every day without one single interruption, whether sick or in health, on the land or on the sea, and whatever the pressure of my engagements might be. Eighteen months elapsed before the first of the five was converted. I thanked God and prayed on for the others. Five years elapsed, and then a second was converted. I thanked God for the second, and prayed on for the other three. Day by day I continued to pray for them, six more years passed before the third was converted. I thanked God for the three, and went on praying for the other two. These two remain unconverted. But I hope in God, I pray on, and look for the answer.'

George Müller had been praying for 36 years for these two individuals. He was 75 years old when he spoke these words. He died in 1898 aged 93. The fourth individual was converted before he died and he died praying for the fifth, 54 years of prayer for one person's salvation. After his death that final person came to faith. By the way, George Müller claimed that he did not have that spiritual gift of special faith, he claimed that it was that ordinary faith given to all Christians.

I have struggled all my life with this issue of reaping. I do not have the gift of evangelism, but I do have a longing, burdened heart. I find it as difficult to approach someone now as ever I did. There are many people I have never approached about the Lord. I read of William Carey's motto, 'Expect great things of God, attempt great things for God,' and am ashamed of the lack of the latter. But I do have a great expectation of God and his willingness and ability to use the most miserable of servants, and despite my limitations he has done so.

Don't be discouraged by the extraordinariness of some of these stories. They are nothing to do with me. If you look carefully it was our great God at work on every occasion and me trying to get my head around what was going on, what he was doing, and how he would have me respond. In the same way as an iceberg is only one quarter visible, there is a far vaster catalogue of failures and missed opportunities on my part, out of view.

I praise God that he is merciful and gracious and kind, and that his blessings have nothing to do with our merit. I think that he responds to our longings not our performance. What is it the psalmist says? 'Delight yourself in the Lord and he will give you the desires of your heart' (Psalm 37:4). If our hearts and minds are focused on him and the things of eternity rather than the things of this world, his spiritual harvest, rather than our material, physical or emotional harvest, we will know times of reaping for which he alone can be given the glory, and times of wonder and joy that no other experience this side of Heaven matches.

Chapter 21

Postscript – It's Not Over Yet

While writing Chapter 14, 'Temporary Freedom', I felt an inner compulsion to re-establish contact with the subject of the chapter, Wayne Hardy, whom I had known in prison and who had 'known' Christ. I didn't know where to start. His home town was Nottingham, but 14 years had passed since he left prison and I had last seen him, so he could have been anywhere, if indeed he was still alive. All I could think to do was to put his name in a search engine in the internet, which I did. His name came up on two sites.

One site was that of Classic Bodybuilders, and I remembered that he had been a bodybuilder, so I went into the site and found a picture of him, all muscle and oil, with his familiar big grin. It was dated 1988, some years before I ever knew him. There was an email contact available, so I emailed the site asking if they could tell me of his whereabouts. I received a rapid, polite response telling me that they no longer had contact with him, with an accompanying list of other bodybuilder sites that might help. I didn't try them as I didn't know if he had continued with his bodybuilding after all these years.

The other site was **www.macintyre.com**, where I discovered that a Donal MacIntyre, an investigative television reporter, had gone undercover in Nottingham ten years ago to investigate the drug-dealing activities of a Wayne Hardy. Donal then screened his findings on the television programme *World In Action*, and Wayne consequently discovered that the man he had trusted had used and betrayed him. He was angry. He wanted revenge. In fact he put a £50,000 price on Donal MacIntyre's head.

I emailed the site in the hope that, despite the film being made so long ago, Donal might point me in the right direction to contact

Wayne. I received no reply. A month later I tried again and Donal MacIntyre's agent replied stating that the previous email to Donal had been, and the present one would be, forwarded to him. Again I heard nothing. I was later to discover that Donal MacIntyre thought my emails were not genuine enquiries, but either a scam by someone claiming to be a Salvation Army officer or a 'nutter'! He could not believe that a Salvation Army officer could really be a friend of Wayne. I later sent a third email and received another assurance that the emails had been passed on to Donal.

Every time I met a stone wall I considered terminating my efforts but, after thought and prayer, I still felt compelled to persist. There was a Salvation Army officer who had lived many years in Nottingham, whom I'd known back when I used to visit Wayne in HMP Lincoln. I decided to telephone him on the off chance that he might have heard of Wayne. He hadn't, but said that he was now responsible for The Salvation Army's community work there and would make enquiries for me among his contacts.

He came back to me the following week to say that there were two criminal brothers named Hardy in the Bakersfield area of Nottingham and one of them might be the man I was seeking. He told me that the last time that one of them appeared in court, the road outside the court had been sealed off and the Hardy in question was transported there under heavy, armed police guard. Also, he told me that one of them had been killed the previous year on Trent Bridge, when he fell under a lorry. I tried ringing the telephone numbers of several community organisations in Bakersfield, which I had found on the internet, and my officer colleague made further enquiries, all without success.

A few weeks later I had to go to Nottingham for a three-day conference. I was disappointed that I had not made any contact with Wayne and was no nearer finding him as I drove into the city. I had wondered whether the Lord was going to bring everything together so that we would have a reunion when I got there. But, as often happens when I am trying to discern what God is doing, I was wrong. However, while there I looked up Hardy in the local telephone directory, although I knew full well Wayne would not have his name and address there. The idea was as daft as looking up CRIMINALS in the yellow pages! There I found the name Hardy twice recorded with a Bakersfield address. I tried telephoning them both, but both numbers were not recognised.

'I bet they are family members who have been put in the telephone directory in error,' I thought to myself. I wrote down the addresses, found the postcodes on the internet when I got home and wrote a letter to each address, enquiring as to whether they were related to or knew of a Wayne Hardy who had lived in the area, enclosing a stamped, addressed envelope in each.

The following Tuesday evening I received a telephone call. It was Wayne himself, as pleased to hear me as indeed I was to hear him. One of my letters had gone to his ex-wife, the other to his mother's previous address, and both had been passed on to him. He also told me of how Donal MacIntyre had asked him if he had any knowledge of a Salvation Army officer who claimed to know him, and discovered that it was true and that Wayne did know me.

Wayne then went on to tell me of his brother Dean being killed on Trent Bridge, his father dying, his 12-year-old terminally ill son and the tragedy of his heroin-addict daughter. He also told me how he and Donal MacIntyre had settled their differences following the *World In Action* film ten years earlier which had resulted in Wayne going to prison for 3½ years, and that Donal was making another documentary about him at this very moment, this time with his approval. He expressed his desire to meet up with me again and I said how I would be more than pleased to meet him again. He then asked me if I would consider taking part in the documentary. I said I would consider it. With the promise to keep in touch with each other we ended the conversation.

I then sent an email to Donal MacIntyre's website/agent:

Dear Sir/Madam,
Please can you let Donal MacIntyre know that I am now in contact with Wayne Hardy.
Thanks & best wishes
Howard P. Webber (Captain)

And I received an email from Donal himself the following day:

> That is fantastic – he has talked fondly of you. He has shown me some of the letters you wrote to him supporting him in tragic times.
> I know he is looking forward to meeting you. And so do I.
> keep well
> Donal

Later that evening another email arrived:

> Dear Mr Webber
> My name is Andrew Swanwick, and I currently work for a company called Dare Films, an independent film company specialising in Crime Documentaries, and run by Donal MacIntyre, a man whom you have recently contacted in relation to Wayne Hardy.
> From speaking to Wayne, I understand that you have recently been in contact with him, and are willing to be interviewed in respect of your dealings with him. We are, as you are no doubt aware, currently making a documentary in relation to Wayne, and are eager to conduct the proposed interview.
> I appreciate that you are a busy man, but would like to invite you to Nottingham on Monday the 5th of March, when we are conducting further filming with Wayne. He is aware of this, and is eager for you to attend. Dare Films will, of course, pay your full expenses for the day, and make a contribution to The Salvation Army for your services.
> Yours faithfully
> Andy Swanwick

So it was that I agreed to take part in the filming. Having informed my headquarters and cleared the Monday to do so, I travelled up to Nottingham on the Sunday afternoon to stay there overnight, staying at the same bed and breakfast that I had stayed at only days previously, when at the conference. There I had shared with the proprietors something of what God is like and what it is to know him and Wayne's story and the fact that I was trying to find Wayne. Imagine their surprise at me returning so soon, having made contact with Wayne and now taking part in a film about him.

On Monday morning Andy Swanwick collected me and took me to Nottingham Prison where they wanted to take some outdoor shots of Wayne. It was great to see him after so many years. They had me pose with him there for a few still shots, and then we both got into a people carrier where we were able to chat together as we travelled to a florist, where Wayne bought flowers, on our way to the local cemetery.

The film crew had to unload all their equipment and set it up, so Wayne and I went to the garden of remembrance where the ashes of Nisha and her daughter Sunnie had been scattered all those years earlier. Wayne replaced the flowers by the commemorative plaque and spoke of his agony and sense of guilt and anger. He spoke of there being no grave, that they didn't each have separate coffins, that he had had no say in any of the funeral arrangements as he was confined to prison when it happened. His grief was tangible.

We then went over to his brother Dean's grave. Wayne had paid for a very large memorial in marble, at least twice the size of a normal plot, no expense spared. The photograph of his brother on the marble headstone bore a striking resemblance to Wayne. Discreet microphones were attached to us at this point and the crew commenced filming as we talked together.

Wayne described how his brother had died as they walked across Trent Bridge. His brother was walking backwards in conversation with Wayne when, not seeing where he was going, he walked into a lamppost, and fell into the road just as a lorry came up and hit him. He just happened to fall the wrong way and died in front of Wayne. They were such close brothers. Wayne still cannot get over it.

The film crew then requested that we walk through the graveyard in conversation while being filmed, before we then returned to the plaque in the garden of remembrance to talk and be filmed and recorded there. There were several times when it felt right to share prayer with Wayne and the camera crew kindly stopped their filming to allow me to do so.

When filming there was completed we were taken to the railway station where, after some guidance from Donal, Wayne and I were filmed in the café area having a conversation. Wayne asked me about how I had come to believe and together we were able to talk to about what happened to him in prison when he invited Christ into his life.

After that we travelled to a tattoo artist, where they filmed Wayne being tattooed. He and I were under the impression it was going to be a brief shot for the camera, showing the large head and shoulders of Jesus on the cross that Wayne already had on his back – something he had had done when he spent two years in South Africa. But they re-tattooed it all – two hours worth! The guys in the tattoo shop and other guys he met outside who were from his world all showed Wayne deference and respect. By the time the tattooist finished Wayne was in pain with a bleeding back and we were all hungry. It was 4 pm, well past lunchtime, and so we travelled to a restaurant. It was a good time of conversation, fun and laughter but, after the meal, while Wayne and Donal were filmed in conversation over a game of pool, I enjoyed a discussion of a spiritual nature with two of the film crew.

We then left the restaurant for our final destination, the flat of Wayne's 24-year-old daughter Kyley. She's a lovely girl, but addicted to heroin. All day she had been in desperate need of a 'fix'. Being there was a heart-rending experience. I felt uncomfortable, because Wayne was very upset and angrily expressed it at one point. One could sense his love for his daughter and his distress, as well as his frustration, anger and sense of helplessness in wanting to help her. The addiction is taking its toll on her health and, without a dramatic turnabout in her situation, there will be but one, inevitable outcome. I left with a very heavy heart, and was returned to my bed and breakfast accommodation to collect my car and drive home.

The film went out on Channel 5 later that year, and there are plans for a worldwide distribution of a longer version. Donal told me that the theme of the film was that of 'redemption', and was to show that, although Wayne's wrong living may have made him rich financially, it had been very costly in personal terms. It would reveal a man who now wants to get things right and make a difference to others so that others will not make the mistakes he has made and that he regrets.

Although he is no longer walking the walk Christ would have him walk and no longer experiences what, for a time, he did when I knew him in prison, there was a remembrance of it and a hankering for it. It was the reason behind him having the large tattoo of the head and shoulders of Christ on the cross tattooed on his back while he was on the run for two years in South Africa. He thought he might feel that nearness again by having him emblazoned on his back, although he knows that the real place for Christ Jesus is in his heart. My continuing prayer is that that will be Wayne's desire again too.

The story hasn't ended.